THE WONDERS OF ITALY

THE WONDERS
OF ITALY

OLIVE COOK

PHOTOGRAPHS BY EDWIN SMITH

A STUDIO BOOK

THE VIKING PRESS · NEW YORK

© 1965 THAMES AND HUDSON LONDON
PUBLISHED IN 1965 BY THE VIKING PRESS, INC.
625 MADISON AVENUE, NEW YORK, N.Y. 10022
LIBRARY OF CONGRESS CATALOG CARD NUMBER: 65-24472
TEXT PRINTED BY EBENEZER BAYLIS AND SON LIMITED WORCESTER ENGLAND
PHOTOGRAVURE PLATES PRINTED BY ETS BRAUN ET CIE MULHOUSE FRANCE
BOUND BY VAN RIJMENAM N.V. THE HAGUE HOLLAND

Contents

Introduction

THE FINEST REWARDS OF SCHOLARSHIP are the fruits of concentration on a particular field, and the trend of our age is towards extreme specialization. A general view is something of a novelty; it demands a certain rashness of spirit but engenders its own peculiar excitement and revelations. The present volume surveys a vast panorama in an effort to see all the contrasting manifestations of the Italian genius as a whole. It suggests a possible coherent approach towards the country which has been the most potent of all influences on the civilization of Europe and which has exerted an irresistible magnetism on northerners from the time when the Venerable Bede made his famous remark: 'Quandiu stat Colysseus, stat et Roma; quando cadet Colysseus cadet Roma, cadet et mundus.'

Travellers of the past tended to pick upon one particular face of Italy, that which most accorded with the interests of their generation. Goethe and Gibbon were most moved by the ruins of antiquity; Claude, Elsheimer, Both, Berchem and Wilson were inspired by the picturesque beauty of the Roman Campagna and of wild lake and mountain landscapes; the Gothic Revival architect Street, who wrote two enthusiastic accounts of his travels in Italy, cared for nothing but medieval buildings, while for the vast majority of 19th and early 20th-century tourists Renaissance Italy overshadowed all other aspects. This book ranges over the whole field, pagan and Christian Italy of all periods except the most recent, though that too inevitably intrudes here and there in the shape of an overhead tangle of wires or of parked motor vehicles. This does not mean that there are no important omissions. Only a fraction of the 'wonders' of which Italy is so prodigal could be included. And apart from one or two of the plates in this preliminary section of the book the photographs have been restricted to works of architecture and art, chosen and arranged in a roughly chronological order in order to highlight the essentials in a pattern which was formed in the classical past and which has recurred under different guises and with varying emphasis ever since. An appreciation of this pattern, however fragmentary, unifies and illuminates not only the monuments recorded here but the background of vivid everyday Italian life against which they appear.

Despite Street's determination to see in it only a Gothic land, the great and abiding attraction of Italy for the north is its fundamentally classical character. The classical or horizontal mode is so much its natural medium of expression that the spire of Tibaldi's S. Gaudenzio at Novara is something of a curiosity and Milan Cathedral with all its show of fretted pinnacles has basically the same shape as a Roman temple. Some of the odd devices and mannerisms Italian architects resorted to in the Middle Ages in their endeavours to reconcile horizontality with the aspiring forms of Gothic are described later. The plan of even the humblest domestic dwellings is governed by this inherent bias (plate 2). The rectangular shape combined with a very low pitched roof is found all over the country with but a single startling exception in Apulia where the 'trulli' (plate 3) are circular in form with a conical roof. In their broad beehive clusters, however, they still make an impression of horizontality.

It was on Italian soil that the art of antiquity survived and it was from Italy that knowledge of it was transmitted to northern Europe. The manner of this survival, the strange repetitions and haunting echoes of classical motifs in Italian art of all periods, the way in which classical forms and attitudes were at first unconsciously absorbed into Christian architecture and design, to be eagerly revived and cherished for their own sake at a later stage, finally becoming the chosen vehicle in a period of enthusiastic religious reform, are the concern of subsequent sections of this book.

A development of this kind is ineluctably attended by duality and contrast and these are part of the fabric of Italian art from the earliest times. The Greek colonists of antiquity were as opposed to the Etruscans in their views of life as disclosed in their surviving monuments as the Early Christians to the ancient Romans, and the Romans synthesized modes of expression as diverse as those represented in these pages by the Byzantine Christ of the Last Judgement at Torcello (plate 51) and the pagan term at Caprarola (plate 93). The state of mind that prompted Hadrian to set up a shrine to Serapis in the seclusion of his country retreat while encouraging the worship of the State gods in Rome by building the Pantheon (plates 22, 23) and commissioning Apollodorus of Damascus to design a Temple of Venus and Rome is exactly paralleled by that which inspired Cardinal d'Este to create his pagan garden within a few miles of Hadrian's Villa, while in Rome he was helping to lay the foundations of a profoundly religious art.

The fascinating and distinguishing feature of contrast in Italy is that while it is always arresting and sometimes even melodramatic, it always evokes a final sensation of harmony, both visually and emotionally. The most familiar of contrasts, the confrontation of pagan and Christian imagery, for instance, reflects an attitude in which classical form and often classical myth and Christian legend are but two aspects of a single reality. The union of pagan and Christian themes in S. Maria dei Miracoli,

Venice (plates 81, 82) is the result of a conscious duality of approach, while the combination in the richly sculptured capitals of the cloister columns of Monreale (plates 45 and 47) of scenes from the New Testament story with such subjects as Mithras sacrificing a bull is an instance of a continuing tradition which permits of contrast without conflict. Where the remains of antiquity and the work of the Christian era are juxtaposed they act as foils to one another but arouse no sense of antagonism. This is the case with the church of S. Nicola, Agrigento, to take but one of many similar instances. Here a Roman temple has become a Christian church with Romanesque arcading across the east end and a Saracenic vault, the whole dominated by the powerful classical cornice of the original sanctuary. Classical calm pervades an interior which despite all its disparate elements gives the impression of an organic growth. Sometimes this feeling of serenity is consciously imparted to a scene of contrast. The confrontation of the ruined Forum and the Colosseum by St Peter's, the most celebrated basilica of Christendom – to take the two images that are associated in every traveller's anticipatory or recollected vision of Rome – is tremendously dramatic, but it exists without visual discord because of the harmonizing effect of Bernini's great colonnade (see plate 4). With its straight entablature and massive scale this majestic work is more closely related to the masterpieces of antiquity than any consciously pagan invention of the Renaissance. Yet Bernini was a deeply religious man and the colonnade is an outstanding instance of the continually recurring fusion in Italian art of Christian fervour with the classical mode.

Many of the contrasts that figure so largely in the Italian scene are enhanced by a talent for dramatic presentation which is as compelling a factor in the pattern of the art and life of the peninsula as its markedly classical propensities. Both features are illustrated by that most individual and conspicuous manifestation of the Italian spirit, the screen frontispiece in church architecture. Each generation of travellers is struck anew by these decorative compositions which are so often unrelated to the structures behind them (see plate 75). The basic shape of their façades derives from the pedimented temple front of classical antiquity and was retained in the Middle Ages in response to an ineradicable preference for the horizontal style in an age when verticality was the order of the day (see page 96). But the dissociation of the frontispiece from the building itself also corresponded to an instinctive aptitude for display, and the screen façade was never abandoned. It became a support for a flourish of ornament, very often of an illusionist character, and an excuse for grand optical inventions like that of Borromini's spectacular façade of S. Agnese, Rome. The screen frontispiece, in short, is symbolic of the Italian genius for scenic effects.

Some of the manifold ways in which this genius has manifested itself from the time of the ancient Romans onwards are described and illustrated in these pages. It is expressed in the remarkable development of perspective painting, the superb art of creating a semblance of reality; it emerges in the addiction to luxurious marble, mosaic, bronze and gilt decoration and in the amazing dexterity of the craftsmen who used the mediums of wood and marble inlay to achieve the most fabulous of all *trompe l'œil* magic (see plate 80). It stimulated the dramatic art of the narrative relief so brilliantly pursued by Roman, medieval, Renaissance and Baroque sculptors and it determined the character of Italian gardens with their theatrical layout and marvellous fantasies of cascade and fountain. It fostered that inclination towards not merely the monumental but the colossal which is so overwhelmingly embodied in buildings such as the Baths of Caracalla and Diocletian, the Pantheon, the Basilica of Maxentius, St Peter's and its Piazza, the Palace at Caserta or the Villa Farnese, Caprarola; and which breaks out in the curious periodic obsession with giants, as exemplified by such divers works as the famous bronze relief of a 'gigantomachia', which once filled the pediment of the Pantheon, Michelangelo's 'David' (plate 83), Rinaldo Mantovano's grotesque frescoes in the Sala dei Giganti at the Palazzo del Te, Mantua, and the terrifying company of rock-cut colossi in the *Sacro bosco* at Bomarzo (plate 92).

The climax and synthesis of all the various aspects of this art of scenic presentation in the magnificent achievement of the Baroque is the subject of the last section of this volume. But this art also permeates the whole spectacle of everyday life in Italy. The very fact that we tend to look upon it as a spectacle is in itself revealing. The shabby grandeur of Italian towns and palaces, the crumbling masonry of picturesque court-yards, the splendidly stagey designs of the great piazzas (see plate 71), are all conceived as backgrounds to the drama of existence. It is more than a coincidence that generations of scene painters have drawn inspiration not only from the famous Italian piazzas but from the no less characteristic alleyway and court, the pictorial essence of which is summed up here in the photograph of S. Angelo Muxaro (plate 1).

Against such grandly contrived backgrounds the Italians go about the business of living and dying with a zest and a complete lack of inhibition which never fail to astound and delight the reticent northerner but which are also part of their genius for display. What else lies behind the consummate artistry shown by street vendors in arranging and disposing of the goods on their barrows, the piled fruit, fish, lace, fountain pens, cheap jewellery or toys? What else prompts the enchanting invention which informs the sugar figures made for the Feast of All Souls or the floral shields carried in funeral and marriage processions? It is a keen sense of drama that promotes the ferocious uproar of the Italian street and piazza, the positive enjoyment of shrill human voices and fevered mechanical noise, the ear-splitting blast of horns, the screech and grind of bus, car and lorry, the waspish drone and splutter of Vespa and Lambretta beyond anything known in other countries. The confrontation of all this animation and high-spirited turmoil with a parade of mortality – the slow passage through the clamorous streets of the ostentatiously gloomy funeral car, sable-plumed, ebony-hued, adorned with flaming urns, extinguished torches and mourning caryatids; the plastering of walls with black-bordered funeral announcements; the exposure in churches of gruesome relics and horrifying images of decay and death – is no less an expression of the Italian's feeling for the dramatic than is his air of unutterable, irredeemable boredom in the provincial piazza on a Sunday afternoon. From Imola in the north to Enna in the south the same scene is enacted. Groups of dark-suited men stand motionless, oblivious of surging traffic, blind altogether to their surroundings, leaning against a balustrade perhaps before some dizzy panorama, or propping themselves against a church wall. Blank, hopeless, they seem neither to expect nor to seek relief from man's predicament in the mass distractions and frenzied tempo of the machine age.

The distinguishing trends in Italian art and life are nourished by the country's geography and geology. No other land is so rich in exotic coloured marbles, and the predilection for sumptuous ornament and magnificent display owes much to this natural and inexhaustible supply of cream and black, flaming red, deep ochre, rose yellow, mottled jade, emerald and moss green, slate-grey, indigo, lilac and purple marble. Contrast is encouraged by the diversity of nature. In the Po valley poplar takes the place of cypress and umbrella pine and points to the difference between this uneventful, trimmed and tamed expanse netted by straight roads, dykes and railways and the desolation of the Roman Campagna or the stony, purple-coloured flats of Apulia. The hills and mountain ranges sweeping down the centre of the narrow peninsula like petrified waves offer a like variety. And this variety is reflected in the continuing use of regional materials down the centuries until the present age of steel and concrete.

The abrupt transitions in the Italian landscape, from monotonous plain to mountain steep and from rounded, gentle, symmetrical hills to high savage plateaux rent by giant fissures and gaping crevices, are mirrored in the contrast between the brick and terracotta of low-lying Lombardy and the limestones of Central Italy. Roman travertine from Tivoli, that uniquely Italian limestone, harmonizes Roman work of all periods, while the diverse colours and textures of the same stone from other quarries give rise to divergencies in the appearance and mood of architecture as exciting as the variations in their natural setting. The honey colour and mellow atmosphere of Rome are entirely opposed to the dark red-brown and brooding spirit of Etruscan Viterbo, Sutri and Tuscania, and both differ from the silvery pallor and tranquillity of Bagnaia and that Arcadian dream of shimmering aigrettes and moving chains of water which is Villa Lante (plates 89–91). Tufa, peperino and lava give unity and vibrancy to the hill towns of the far south and to cities such as Naples, Bari, Palermo and Catania. These volcanic stones are eloquent of the enduring menace of Vesuvius and Etna and of the towering, unquiet mountain landscapes of Calabria where infinite recessions of lurching, toppling crags are veined with gleaming quartz and melodramatically illumined by sudden shafts of light. The 'wonders' shown in these pages are historic and it is historic Italy which is the principal goal of both traveller and aesthete. But to many of the Italians themselves the past is an incubus and the prevailing atmosphere in which its relics are now seen is vastly different from the cosy, infinitely congenial Italy of the Brownings,

George Eliot and Henry James. The whole peninsula is rapidly changing under the impact of industrialization. The destruction of the Italian landscape is proceeding with characteristic Italian abandon and at a more furious rate and with less protest than anywhere else in Europe. The south has already undergone a transformation so great that Norman Douglas would now scarcely recognize the remote towns he describes in *Old Calabria*. Factories and featureless apartment blocks encircle medieval hill towns and stretch for mile after mile in plain and valley. The flat lands behind Ravenna and Rimini and the environs of Venice have become industrial infernos of unrivalled ugliness; the coasts, once unsurpassed, are now almost totally ruined. These developments and the impact of Italy's millions of tourists may well before very long render the pleasures of contemplation obsolete and place insuperable obstacles in the way of any photographer who wishes to record the visible foundations of the history and art of Europe.

Meanwhile the masterpieces which for so many centuries have drawn men south from their northern homelands continue to inspire the admiration and exhilaration which countless poets, painters, historians, archaeologists and scholars of other ages have felt in their presence. They are still a superlative source of delight and invention, they dominate the trivial, expendable products of the present just as the peerless achievements of the pagan world towered above the uniformity, the regimentation and materialism of the last years of the Roman Empire.

Since this remote mountain village is situated on a spur of rock some 8,000 feet high, the long main street terminating in a piazza usual to Sicily is replaced by a central square with irregular courtyards. The photograph shows a ruinous, picturesque corner with speckled hens clucking about the doorways and lines of washing strung from wall to wall, that is characteristically Italian; but the rough stone paving interrupted here and there by glittering quartz is peculiar to the height and geographical position of this wild, inaccessible place. S. Angelo Muxaro was the site of a large prehistoric settlement and the mountain-side falling away immediately behind this courtyard is pierced by fifty or more domed and rock-cut tombs.

1
S. ANGELO
MUXARO,
SICILY

About a century ago, when the danger of attack by bandits no longer threatened, the old town on the summit of a steep, conical hill from where this photograph was taken was abandoned by the inhabitants for the more convenient site of the present settlement along the banks of a sluggish river. The low-pitched roofs and basic rectangular plans of the huddled houses may be found anywhere in Italy; it is the landscape that is peculiarly Sicilian. Bare, bony, chalk-white crags burst from lion-coloured earth, blotched with fennel, carob trees and prickly pears, pitted by tombs and torn by deep gullies, the stony beds of winter torrents.

2
MONTALLEGRO,
SICILY

The entire town of Alberobello consists of the circular, domed houses known as 'trulli', only to be found in this corner of Apulia. They dot the flat landscape in clusters of from three to four or occasionally as many as seven or eight, and at Alberobello crowd together on a gentle slope, all painted white. The majority of the examples date from

3
ALBEROBELLO,
APULIA
VIA D'ANNUNZIATA

the 17th and 18th centuries. No satisfactory reason has yet been advanced for this strange plan, though a circular design is well adapted to a structure of dry stone walling, eliminating as it does the need for quoins. The origins of this indigenous style may perhaps be akin to those which inspired the very similar prehistoric fortress dwellings of the Sardinians. Except for a few farms along the great Campigna ridge above the plain behind Ravenna, built of limestone with stone slate roofs, the 'trulli' provide the only instances in the whole of the peninsula of departure from the universal use in Italy of tiles for roofs.

4
ROME
PIAZZA S. PIETRO:
BERNINI'S
COLONNADE

The photograph shows the wonderfully sculptural and powerful effect of Bernini's massive free-standing columns of travertine. His design for the Piazza was begun in 1656 and underwent several changes before it assumed its present aspect eleven years later. Bernini had intended to enclose the Piazza by linking the two long colonnades but the plan was never carried out owing to the death in 1667 of his patron Alexander VII. See also pages 11 and 195.

5
FLORENCE FROM
S. MINIATO AL
MONTE

Florence is especially a Renaissance city although it stands above a sunken Roman town. Roman Florence survives in a few street names such as Via delle Terme and Via del Campidoglio and the plan of the Roman colony which replaced an Etruscan settlement in the first century AD can still be dimly discerned in the layout of modern Florence, but there are no Roman ruins above ground. Until the 12th century Fiesole was a more important centre than Florence. The prospect of the city from S. Miniato al Monte began to assume its present appearance in the early 14th century and has changed very little since Brunelleschi added his great dome to the cathedral in 1461. The adjacent campanile which rises conspicuously beside the west front of the church was designed by Giotto in 1334, continued by Andrea Piccino from 1336 to 1348 and completed by Talenti a few years later. The tower of the Palazzo Vecchio with its battlements and machicolations, which after the dome is the most prominent and characteristic feature in the landscape, is traditionally ascribed to Arnolfo di Cambio (1298–1314).

6
VENICE
PIAZZA S. MARCO

As with the preceding view of Florence dominated by Brunelleschi's dome, familiarity can never dull the magical effect of this great piazza and the startling novelty of its images: the broad level space, where there are no vehicles of any kind, the immense campanile and the long, low, fairy-tale shape of St Mark's closing the vista. This façade, with its unparalleled wealth of shafts below, encrusted with the richest marbles, mosaics, statuary and gilding, surmounted by ogee gables extravagantly crocketed and by a cluster of oriental domes, is so full of incongruities and improbable juxta-positions that it bursts upon the eye like a fantastic dream miraculously translated into stone. It is an extreme expression of the harmonious reconciliation of contrasts, of the love of display and the fundamental horizontality which characterize Italian art everywhere.

St Mark's stands on the site of the original basilican church founded in AD 864 to receive the body of the saint. The plan was entirely altered between 1042 and 1085 and assumed the Byzantine form of a Greek cross with domes. The façade dates mostly from the 12th century.

The paved Piazza, which like the Forum of ancient Rome is the centre of city life, assumed its definitive form in the 15th century. It was originally the site of a convent garden but ceased to be used as such when the space became necessary for the gathering of the people for the *arengo*, the method by which the Venetians elected the Doge.

The campanile was begun by Doge Giovanni Partecipazio towards the end of the 10th century, but it was not actually erected until the 12th. Repeated damage by light-ning weakened the structure and eventually caused the whole building to collapse in 1902. It was rebuilt in 1912 exactly as it had been before the disaster.

Plates 1-6

The Pagan World

To some extent, we can still share the picturesque and poetic attitude of our forefathers to the fabulous remains of antiquity in Italy. Despite the intensive cleaning, clearing, de-mossing and labelling activities of the present century, they are as eloquent as ever they were of the greatness of vanished civilizations and the inevitable end of all fabrics and all human institutions. But the archaeological approach is more in key with the temper of today and, with the ever-growing number of new discoveries and the increasingly precise classification of existing material, it must now enter into any consideration of the classical past from whatever angle it is regarded. It certainly plays its part in illuminating one of the most fascinating of all the aspects of pagan art in Italy – the way in which it influenced and anticipated, not only the styles but the spirit of everything that came later. The seeds of all the aesthetic movements and all the tremendous oscillations in attitude which accompanied them, from Early Christian times, when the memory of Greece and Rome was still strong to the Baroque period, are to be found in classical antiquity itself. It was in pagan Italy that the stage was set for all future developments and it was against the dramatic backcloth of pagan ruin that the distinguishing characteristic of Italian art of all periods – which may perhaps be summed up as a genius for display – was unfolded. It is a story of fascinating influences and affinities that ends only with the fancy-dress and lifeless art of Italian Neo-classicism. Part of this story will form the subject of subsequent sections of this book; the present few pages are concerned principally with an evocation of the classical sources for what followed.

The traditional date of the foundation of Rome was 753 BC and in the course of that century Greek colonists had established themselves in Italy, while the Etruscans, who had probably settled on the peninsula considerably before that period, were trading regularly with the Greeks by the beginning of the 7th century BC. The Romans were exposed very early to Hellenic influence and the Etruscans were closely involved in the primitive history of Rome. There were supposedly even Etruscan kings of Rome – Tarquinius the Elder, who was of Greek ancestry, Servius Tullius and Tarquinius Superbus. When, therefore, the Romans attained their final supremacy, the mosaic of art and the varieties of thought and feeling they transmitted to the later Italians were composed of strands which men had been weaving together for centuries.

The connection between the South of Italy and Greece goes back at least to about 1200 BC and memories of the Myceneans in Sicily and on the mainland survive in the tales of the wanderings of Odysseus. This colonizing dates from the 8th century BC when Greeks were leaving their native land for reasons of trade and over-population. Their principal settlements were Cumae, Posidonia (Paestum), Sybaris, Croton, Locri, Tarentum and Rhegium on the mainland and Naxos, Leontine, Catane, Zancle (Messina), Syracuse, Megara Hyblaea, Gela, Akragas (Agrigento), Selinus (Selinunte) and Himera in Sicily. The Greek colonial temples (plates 7–10) are grander and more impressive than those of Greece itself and they are most interestingly different from them. They are all in the Doric style and are fashioned of the local stone instead of the marble always used by the Greeks in their homeland. The coarse travertine of which the temples at Paestum are built has weathered to a wonderfully intense orange colour; the limestone of Selinunte is like the palest honey, that of Syracuse resembles bleached bone, while the ruins of Agrigento are of tawny sandstone. In every case the fossil shells and small aqueous plants embedded in the masonry impart an enchanting sense of life and variety to the texture. This, of course, remarkably attractive though it is, is only an effect of ruin, for the Greeks attached so much importance to the quality of their fine-grained marble that they coated the Italian temples with stucco, flakes of which still occasionally adhere to the flutes of the columns.

The temples are strongly individual in character and some of them show features found nowhere else. In the Paestum temples, especially the 'Basilica' (plate 9), *entasis* (the gradual tapering both upwards and downwards from a carefully calculated height), introduced by the Greeks to counter the waisted look of straight-sided columns, is used so obtrusively that the result is grotesque, almost as if the architect had not understood the purpose of the device. This building boasts another unusual feature in the ornament on the necking of the huge columns. The internal colonnade of the 'Temple of Poseidon', surmounted by smaller Doric columns (plate 7), exhibits an arrangement unique of its kind. A possible explanation of this upper colonnade (this is only a suggestion) is that the Romans may have been responsible for it. Their basilicas exhibit exactly similar arrangements and with their strong antiquarian interests they may well have adapted this temple for their own purposes, retaining the original Doric style, when Paestum became a Roman town. The ruins of this town, the Forum, streets and the foundations of houses planned like those of Pompeii, lie adjacent to the temples, and it is highly significant that the remains of the columns of the Roman Forum are of the Doric order.

A unique design occurs also in the Temple of Zeus, Agrigento (Akragas): the figures of giants, companions of the survivor shown lying among the fragments of the shattered shrine in plate 10, were used as structural supports in the outer screen walls. No temple in Greece equalled this vast structure in size and in Sicily it was surpassed only by the greatest of the temples at Selinunte (Selinus). The remains show that its builder, traditionally Theron, departed radically from Greek principles of construction, for half-columns, architrave and mouldings were all composed of small pieces of stone instead of single blocks.

Not only does the work of the Greek colonists in Italy differ structurally from that in their homeland, but the dedications of the temples, where they are known, point to the association of special divinities with the colonies. The beautiful myth of the goddesses of the earth that sent up the fruitful corn existed in Sicily and on the mainland long before the Greeks established themselves there. The newcomers embroidered this myth with a story of their own, and the Sicilian Hybla and the Campanian Ceres became identified with Demeter. The goddess Ceres of the Roman pantheon only took on the importance she later assumed as a result of this amalgamation. From the time of Pindar, Demeter and Persephone were regarded as the particular patronesses of Sicily. Temples and shrines to these two divinities are a common feature of the Greek settlements, and at Megara Hyblaea Demeter was still worshipped under her Sikelian name of Hybla. The northernmost temple at Paestum has always been regarded as sacred to Demeter and the recent discovery of a subterranean shrine of Persephone beside the main building with a vase inscribed 'I am sacred to the nymph' confirms the tradition. Some thirty years ago a shrine of Persephone was discovered at Agrigento, below the church of San Biagio which incorporates a Doric temple of Demeter. It is reached by rock-cut steps in the side of a ravine above the dry bed of the river Akragas. The foundations of the sanctuary can be made out beside aqueducts and fountains, whose rectangular basins still stand, and the sweet, purling sound of running water can still be heard there, a rare and welcome omen of spring in arid Agrigento.

A sanctuary of Demeter is one of the few identified temples at Selinunte, and the legend of corn and fruitfulness emphasizes the desolation of this place today. It is worth a brief description, for it is perhaps the only antique ruin in Italy that can be enjoyed in anything approaching the conditions in which our forefathers saw it. The gigantic fragments lie in the wildest disarray on either side of a shallow valley in a plateau which stretches bleakly to the horizon. One or two isolated decapitated columns still stand upright in the chaos, but these and the shafts and architrave of a portico only emphasize the confusion of the scene. Parts of massive cornices, fluted pillars so great of girth it seems impossible they could be the work of men, cover the ground in disorder, their likeness to immense rocks enhanced by the coarseness of the stone and by the cavernous recesses and piled eminences formed by the ruins. The mystery which shrouds these mighty remains has never been satisfactorily solved. Some say the temples were destroyed by the Phoenicians, who twice sacked the city, once in 409 and again in 250 BC; others that no power less than an earthquake could have dislodged these countless blocks of masonry and thus tossed and scattered them as though they were no more than leaves.

Not only is the cause of the catastrophe uncertain but, as has already been mentioned, the temples, apart from the shrine of Demeter, have not been identified. Modern archaeologists recognize them by alphabetical labelling. Their work at Selinunte provoked an angry outburst from Gregorovius when he visited the ruins in 1886: they had wantonly destroyed the savage poetry of the site, he said. If he could return now he would be comforted to find that vegetation once more clothes the fallen masonry, that the shepherd, clasping, it is true, a bushy umbrella instead of a crook, once again drives his flock along a sandy rut beneath great overhanging masses of stone and blackens overthrown columns with his evening fire; and if the spotted snake so dear to the German historian no longer breeds in the ruins, lizards and adders by the dozen bask on the former altars.

Syracuse, more than any other of the Greek colonies in Italy, is haunted by the heroic past: it was the birthplace of Archimedes and Theocritus, the refuge of Aeschylus until he settled in Gela, and the scene of important episodes in the life of Euripides. Under Dionysius Syracuse became one of the greatest Greek states, second in influence to Sparta alone and larger than Athens. This period of splendour was preceded by one of the most spectacular events in ancient history, the defeat of the Athenian fleet under Alcibiades in the Great Harbour. Nearly two hundred ships were engaged while spectators lined the basin of the harbour or watched from the upper plateau of Epipolae. The destruction of the fleet was followed by the surrender of the Athenian army, fatal blows to the power of Athens. This epic history is illumined by impressive architectural remains. There is the great Doric shrine of Athene which now encloses the cathedral with its Baroque façade (plate 14); one of the grandest of all the Greek theatres, at Epipolae (plate 11), commands the scene of the Greek defeat; and there are the Latomie dei Capucini, the quarries that supplied the stone for the Greek and Roman monuments of Syracuse. The pale stone has been quarried down to a depth of a hundred or more feet, making sheer cliffs on every side. It was here that the Syracusans imprisoned some seven hundred Athenians after their victory of 413 BC. One strange grotto, deep and high and hewn in the form of the letter 'S', intensifies the sinister aspect of this exotic place; it has curious acoustic properties, for it echoes the lightest whisper. It is known as the 'Ear of Dionysius' and is an apt symbol of the tyrant's power. Among the Roman buildings of Syracuse there are two of great interest which show marked Greek influence, the Gymnasium in the modern quarter of the town, a grandiose structure including a theatre and a temple of simplicity rare in Roman architecture, and the enchanting amphitheatre close to the Greek theatre. It belongs to the 3rd century AD and is therefore later than the Colosseum, but it follows the style of its neighbour very closely even in the lettering on the rock-cut seats. The Greek theatre was altered by the Romans in accordance with the requirements of their drama, which developed on quite different lines from that of the Greeks. The centre of this theatre was originally a complete circle for the orchestra in which the chorus chanted and danced, while the stage was a narrow platform with a low architectural background. The Romans reduced the central circle to half its area and also restricted the auditorium which, when it was first constructed, encircled at least two-thirds of the orchestra.

The Theatre at Taormina (plate 12) has been even more radically changed. The auditorium is still further restricted, though it is brought into immediate connection with the stage; the stage itself has been heightened and the architectural background – the prototype of the fixed perspective scenery of Palladio's Teatro Olimpico (plate 96) – is far more developed.

The remains of the Greek colonists are conspicuous and unforgettable images in the landscape of southern Italy. The architecture of the Etruscans, which so greatly influenced not only Roman practice but through Roman interpretation that of the whole future development of building construction, has almost entirely vanished. A few fragments of masonry remain – the cyclopean, dry stone jig-saw walls of Perugia and Alatri, the Cloaca Maxima (the oldest example of true arch construction in Europe, built to drain the valleys between the hills of Rome), the watercourses at Porto San Clementino near Tarquinia and running from Lago Burano to Cosa, the amphitheatre at Sutri (plate 15), and one or two bridges rebuilt by the Romans. But nothing else survives above ground to bear witness to the profound impact of the mysterious people who almost succeeded in unifying the peninsula before they were overcome by the Romans. They are known to us chiefly through their tombs and their burial rites. Everything has conspired to envelop them in obscurity. An Etruscan grammar and history compiled by the Emperor Claudius were lost and the language of the people, an understanding of which would probably explain their origin, remains an enigma. There are two conflicting views about the Etruscans both of which date from antiquity. Herodotus declared that they were an oriental race, Lydians, driven from their own country by famine in the 13th century BC, while Dionysius of Halicarnassus, a Greek living in Rome under Augustus, maintained that they were an ancient indigenous people whose language and religious beliefs showed that they could have nothing in common with the Lydians. Modern scholarship favours the first alternative. But the whole subject is still a matter of endless debate.

Whatever their origin, the Etruscans were firmly established in Italy, as we have seen, by the early 8th century BC and in estimating their prodigious influence it must be remembered that in the early days of the Roman Empire Etruscan literature was still being read and Etruscan works on the all-important topics of mensuration and engineering were still in use. Etruscan persisted as a language of the priests and was current in Roman temples. Roman connoisseurs collected Etruscan works of art; and Roman comedy derived entirely from Etruscan example, if we are to believe Livy, who also relates that Etruscan dancers and flautists were brought to Rome during an epidemic of the plague in the hope of appeasing the gods. After the fall of Rome all interest in the Etruscans lapsed; the part they had played in Roman art and life was forgotten and the very memory of their existence grew faint. But during the Middle Ages the famous Capitoline Wolf was discovered, and the Arezzo Chimaera, the Minerva, the Orator and a great many smaller bronzes were unearthed in the 16th century, when they aroused tremendous excitement. The Chimaera was restored by Cellini. During the first half of the 18th century Volterra was excavated and from then onwards, as one remarkable discovery followed another, scholars became obsessed with the idea of penetrating the Etruscan mystery. Tombs were examined systematically at Tarquinia, Vulci, Chiusi, Vetulonia and Orvieto and as more and more remains came to light — the most celebrated of all the Etruscan sarcophagi, that of Cerveteri, now in the Louvre; the monumental statue of Mars found near Todi; the astonishing series of life-size terracottas at Veii, including the unforgettable, vigorous Apollo with his bold gaze and predatory smile — so a body of knowledge was gradually amassed about the lives of this vanished race. The fact that their actual history remains obscure lends added fascination to the full details which the tombs of the Etruscans have revealed about their habits and beliefs. Their dress, their favourite adornments, all the oddities of their toilet, their sports and pastimes, their gay banquets, the houses they inhabited, the furniture they used, their marriage and funeral rites, their religious observances, even the adventures of their souls in the world to come, all are depicted in the paintings on the walls of their tombs, on their sarcophagi and on their cinerary urns. Most dramatic and moving of all, their peculiar physiognomy is as vividly known to us as that of our living acquaintances through their remarkable funerary portrait figures. The strong faces of the Etruscan men and women reclining on their tombs in the rooms and courtyard of the Gothic Palazzo Vitelleschi in Tarquinia are unforgettable. They lie as at a banquet, singly and in couples, proud, sombre, alert, wide-eyed. Modern Tarquinia is built on the hill consecrated by the Etruscans to the dead and the dead still dominate this walled town with its tiara of fantastic towers. The presence of these people in fact still haunts the whole territory between Orvieto, Viterbo and Tarquinia, a territory of desolate tablelands, criss-crossed by deep, rust-coloured gorges forming the lofty, inaccessible promontories upon which the Etruscans preferred to build their towns. A favourite position was the junction of two ravines, as at Sutri, standing on a rocky islet, or Tuscania, a small battlemented town constructed of the same brown tufa as the hill on which it rises. The hill is an island in a narrow valley the sides of which are vertical cliffs sheltering the town so effectively from sight that its presence only becomes known a few yards from the gate. On one of the walls surrounding the main square the moss-stained figures of dead Etruscans lie on the lids of their sarcophagi, keeping a curious watch on the lives of their descendants and successors, and there is an indescribable excitement in such chance encounters with these inscrutable people.

The superb Roman synthesis of the Etruscan themes of arch, vault and dome with the architectural orders and the trabeated style of the Greeks is a concrete manifestation of an attitude to life which likewise derived mainly from these two great sources of inspiration and was to prove of the utmost significance for the future of Italian art. The Romans are generally thought of as an intensely practical people who experienced no mystic urge to worship superhuman powers. Their official gods, most of whom were either directly taken over from Greek mythology or transformed by Greek influence, were regarded as protectors who responded to correctly performed observances; and their public worship was eventually only kept up as a matter of State policy. But a confused version of the terrifying religion of the Etruscans, which was basically oriental in character, lived on in the Roman conception of the infernal regions. Characteristics of the dread Etruscan demons Charun, Tuchulcha and Geryon, and of the Etruscan belief in an after-life and in good and evil genii who struggled for the possession of the soul at the moment of death, survived in the Roman Manes, Orcus, Februs and Dis Pater. Etruscan gods such as the Lar, who was originally associated with the under-world, played a part in the all-important private cults of the Romans. In every Roman house there were altars to the deities of the hearth and home who were not of Greek derivation but who belonged to the most ancient Italic mythology. In these private cults a genuine religious sense persisted and they prepared the way for the Roman acceptance during the later stages of their history of the religions of the East, of the cults of the great Phrygian goddess Cybele, of the Egyptian Isis and Serapis and, most important of all, of the Persian Mithras, whose worship had so much in common with the Christianity which in the end conquered the Roman world.

We are closer, and not only in time, to the Romans than to the Greek colonizers or the Etruscans. The events of Roman history often seem less distant than those of the Middle Ages and the appearance of Roman monuments has been familiar to us from childhood, not only through pictures of Rome but through examples of Roman architecture in northern lands and wherever Roman government extended. The Romans' methods of construction and the materials they used; their brilliant exploitation of brick and concrete, light plastic materials that enabled them to enclose vast covered spaces and support huge vaults; their sense of spatial design, and the great scale and sheer grandeur of their work are all of exceptional interest to this age of steel and concrete building. But even more than these most significant features of Roman architecture, it is the daily life of the ancient Romans that fascinates us today. The Doric temples of the Greek colonists speak of gods and heroes, of a life incredibly distant and different from our own; the attraction of the Etruscans lies in the mystery that divides us from them and we know them only through the trappings and rites of death; but the Romans are revealed to us in the fullness of life, firstly through the remains of their public buildings and secondly through their houses and the survival of all the actual appurtenances of their domesticity.

The ruined Forums of the Romans (see plates 20 and 28), especially the Forum Romanum with its complex of temples, basilicas, public buildings, shops and markets, are still eloquent of the pulsating corporate life of the city which once filled them. Their Thermae, those most characteristic of Roman buildings, still speak of the manners and customs of a pleasure-loving people. For the Thermae were not only designed for luxurious bathing with the attendance of anointers, manicurists, barbers, shampooers and hundreds of slaves, but were resorted to for news and gossip, for lectures and athletic sports, and indeed wealthy Romans spent a great part of their day in these club-like institutions. The Thermae of Caracalla, with accommodation for 1,600 bathers, give us, even in their ruined state, a splendid idea of the size and magnificence of such establishments. Here it is still possible to trace the layout of the *tepidarium*, or warm lounge, the *calidarium* or hot room with a hot bath, the *sudatorium* (sweating-room), the *frigidarium* with its swimming bath, the dressing-rooms, libraries and lecture halls. In their immensity these Thermae surpass the most gigantic works of later ages: the majestic rhythm of the changing vistas unfolded by the series of vast halls and saloons already states the theme of the monumental vestibule at Caserta; while the sumptuous ornament which once covered walls, floor and ceiling, the richly coloured marbles, the mosaics, the gilded coffers and paintings reflect that same gift for scenic presentation which prompted the ornate interior of the Royal Palace at Turin, the façade of S. Michele, Lucca (plate 57) or the interior of S. Ivo della Sapienza, Rome.

Stirring to the imagination as are these great Thermae, deeply moving as are the broken columns, the fragmentary though magnificent arcades, the terraces and the rugged masonry identified by archaeologists as the temples, libraries, porticos, baths and halls of the palaces of the Caesars on the Palatine Hill, it is only in the mind's eye that these arrogant structures take on the full-blooded life of which they were a part. Ruined Ostia, despite its skeleton warehouses, granaries and homes of wealthy merchants, makes a mournful impression of a city abandoned to slow decay – and it was indeed gradually deserted by its inhabitants owing to the ravages of malaria. Hadrian's great sprawling villa at Tivoli (plate 42) and the palatial residence of an unknown Roman connoisseur at Piazza Armerina (plate 41) do indeed create an extraordinarily vivid sense of luxurious living.

Yet if these were the only Roman dwellings to survive, our contact with their owners would still be largely the work of fantasy. It is the discovery of Pompeii and Herculaneum which has animated the whole Roman world for us and made us intimately aware of the daily lives of the people. These small provincial towns differed vastly, of course, from Rome itself, not only in size but in their material and social aspects; but they belonged to the same civilization and the lives of their inhabitants were much the same as those of other members of the Empire. It is possible here to study the private houses of the ancients in all their forms and evolutionary stages. The earliest houses, like the House of the Surgeon at Pompeii, consisted of an atrium with rooms grouped round it and a small garden at the back. The garden later became the peristyle, a formal plot surrounded by colonnades with rooms opening on to it from all sides. Most houses were occupied by only one family, but there were also a few apartment houses, such as later became extremely common in Roman cities. Roman houses faced inwards, not towards the street, and one of the first peculiarities to strike a visitor to Pompeii is the contrast between the grim, austere street wall and the gaiety and refinement of the inside rooms. Scarcely a single window in the whole town looks on to the street. Inside the house, air and light penetrated through doorways into the two central open spaces, the atrium and the peristyle; and frescoes took the place of views through windows. The rooms were usually on one floor only and each room was intended for one purpose only.

The wonder of Pompeii and Herculaneum is that they are not, like all the other ruins of antiquity, merely the shells left by the life that once warmed them; they still overflow with the suddenly arrested and miraculously preserved life that pulsated there on the day of the catastrophe which buried them. The abrupt and terrible destruction of these towns has always exercised an irresistible appeal as an illustration of the uncertainty and fragility of life, but the surprising story of the recovery of the cities, a story that is still unfolding as year by year fresh houses, gardens, temples and theatres are disinterred, is still more moving and almost as dramatic. More and more about the last moments in the lives of the citizens is being revealed, and at Herculaneum, scarcely touched during previous centuries, houses are coming one by one to light in which every object remains as it was left on 24 August AD 79, the date of the calamity. Eggs, nuts, fruit and grain stand in the larders, bread is ready to be taken from the oven, the pot stands on the stove, the strainer close at hand, the library shelves are full of charred papyrus rolls, the sealed containers let into the counters of the taverns still contain the dregs of the wine that filled them, a shovel leans against a boiler door, a table is still laid with a modest lunch: eggs, still in their shells, cake and bread rolls.

The vibrating humanity of these doomed people is not only present in details such as these, it is touchingly displayed in hundreds of inscriptions scratched on the surface of plaster and painted on walls in Pompeii. Some of these inscriptions advertise houses and land for sale or to let, others announce the programmes of concerts and spectacles or name the candidates for forthcoming municipal elections. There are many others of a more intimate character – shop accounts, lists of gambling debts, the scribbles of schoolboys, the threats and insults of tramps and vagabonds, lovers' protestations and many obscenities, crude expressions of dionysiac exuberance which facetious guides are at pains to screen from modest 'signore'. Sometimes the infuriated owners of houses whose walls had been defaced with graffiti would cover them with an inscription of their own, prohibiting further outrage and calling down the wrath of Pompeian Venus on all who infringed the prohibition. So far no such inscriptions have been discovered at Herculaneum. Only a single scribble has come to light, on the lavatory wall of the House of the Gem. The passing visit of a famous doctor is commemorated by this vivid sentence: 'Apollinaris medicus Titi imperatoris hic cacavit bene.'

The minuteness and clarity of the image of the daily life of the Romans revealed by Pompeii and Herculaneum gives this encounter with the classical past something of the quality of a particularly graphic dream. And the dream-like impression is enhanced as one walks along the ghostly streets, paved, grooved with deep wheel ruts and crossed by high stepping-stones, and looks into houses and baths and shops, by the sense of familiarity aroused by the character of Pompeian design. Robert and James Adam and their contemporaries in France and Germany drew the inspiration for the decorative details of their work very largely from Pompeii; their furniture, lion-footed and supported by sphinxes, their elegant stucco work and painted ornament, the enchanting patterns which enliven their doorways and fanlights, all echo motifs found at Pompeii. This was a direct and definite influence following on the amazing discoveries made during the 18th century. But there is something uncanny about the strange parallels between Pompeian work and that of artists who knew nothing of it. The stucco panelling of the Thermae at Herculaneum, exposed only in recent years, differs from Pompeii in just the same way as Wyatt's interiors differ from those of Adam: they are less crowded, less fussy, consisting of plain rectangles adorned with single, isolated reliefs. Wyatt had visited Pompeii, but he could never have set eyes on the Thermae, where the ornament and its disposition are fantastically like those at Heveningham. The paintings on the walls of Pompeian and Herculanean houses seem to foreshadow all later developments of the art in Europe. They include landscapes, still lifes, flower and animal pictures, portraits, mythological and genre subjects, treated in every conceivable manner, linear and decorative, painterly and boldly modelled, classic and romantic, factual and fanciful, realistic and impressionistic. Even *trompe l'œil* and abstract painting are found at Pompeii and the present fashion for combining different materials in a non-figurative composition have their prototypes in the Pompeian artists' use of stucco, paint, marbling and mosaic to create varying textures in an abstract pattern. Renoir likened the Pompeian painting he saw in Naples to Corot: 'Those priestesses in their silver-grey tunics could be absolutely taken for Corot nymphs,' he wrote. In the same way intimations of the work of Guardi, G. D. Tiepolo, Raphael, Caravaggio, Claude, Poussin, Ingres, Fragonard or Hubert Robert everywhere create a sense of precognition in the small rooms of the Pompeian houses. The fresco of Flora in the Naples Museum and the elongated Venus in her shell, one of the latest discoveries at Pompeii, are so close in both style and theme to Botticelli, that it seems unbelievable he could never have seen them. Still more curious is the inexplicable resemblance between the composition and subject matter of Giorgione's enigmatical *Tempesta* and a Pompeian fresco, the iconography of which, like that of the Venetian picture, remains completely obscure. The two paintings are even alike in colour and differ only in the treatment of the background and the fact that the groups of figures are reversed: in the Pompeian composition the woman sits on the left. The extravagances of Baroque architecture and the décor of the Bibbiena are alike foreshadowed by a wall decoration at Herculaneum which shows a grandiloquent architectural fantasy presented with every trick of perspective and illusionism. An elaborate doorway surmounted by broken pediments, masks and asymmetrical arches gives on to a fabulous receding vista of colonnades, pilasters and gigantic cornices, and this is framed by ornate pillars and a curtain like the proscenium of a theatre.

A short account of the unique story of Pompeii, unique not only in Italy but in the whole world, does not seem out of place here. The original inhabitants of the Campanian cities were Oscans. They were conquered successively by the Etruscans and the Samnites, and they fought with the Samnites against Rome. But in 290 BC they became subject allies of Rome and by 80 BC they were completely Romanized. In AD 62 there occurred an earthquake which had caused considerable destruction in both Pompeii and Herculaneum. The Pompeian house of the banker Lucius Caecilius Jucundus is adorned with a relief showing the Temple of Jupiter with the adjacent triumphal arch in the Forum and the Vesuvian Gate all collapsing during the earth's convulsion. Seventeen years later the volcano, which had shown no sign of activity within living memory and was clad almost to the summit with vineyards, awoke and to the accompaniment of a fearful clap of thunder, split open. Fire broke from its heart, to be instantly followed by an immense cloud of black smoke which Pliny the Younger, who was watching the phenomenon from the Roman naval base sixteen miles away, likened to the form of an umbrella pine, the sinister shape we have come to associate with atomic explosions. Showers of cinders and ashes began to fall with the fury of the great primordial cataclysms of the earth, and the sun was wholly obscured.

This was the fearful eruption which Pliny the Younger described so vividly in his famous letter to Tacitus, and in which his Uncle Pliny the Elder lost his life. The last moments of many of the victims have been grimly chronicled by their own buried remains. The Pompeians who fled when the ashes began to fall met their death on the roads leading to Stabiae or Nuceria; those who sought refuge in the cellars of their houses were suffocated by the sulphurous fumes that infected the air. In Herculaneum the situation was different. The town escaped the rain of ashes and the poisonous exhalations blown by the north-west wind upon Pompeii. But it lay only two miles from the crater and almost at once an avalanche of lava advanced upon the town. It rolled on, reaching in places a height of thirty to forty feet and covered houses, temples and theatres, tearing down statues, filling cellars, sometimes carrying away walls with it; leaving Herculaneum, as it cooled, completely hidden and encased in the hardest stone. In face of that inexorable stream the inhabitants fled without attempting to save their possessions, and most of them escaped with their lives. When at last day dawned again on the stricken towns, the whole landscape within a radius of twenty miles of Vesuvius was nothing but a blackened heap of cinders and lava. The shape of the volcano was transformed: its former conical tip had vanished and a light cloud of white smoke hovered above an entirely new peak.

The tops of the taller Pompeian buildings still showed above their ashy blanket and soon the few survivors crept back to salvage what they could. They managed to penetrate parts of the Forum and they removed pictures and statues. Herculaneum, stonily sealed, could not be touched, and in time a village grew up immediately above it. When all that was visible of the roofs and towers of Pompeii had been quarried away the city sank and was quite hidden by layer upon layer of vegetation, wild scrub, coarse grass and vineyards. The very sites of the antique towns were almost forgotten, although the city status of Pompeii was vaguely commemorated by the local name of Civitas and stories of buried treasure continued to be told about the Vesuvian landscape; while in the popular imagination the gods, whose deeds were recorded in hundreds of vivid paintings and sculptures beneath the ground, haunted the mountain in the guise of ghosts and demons.

For hundreds of years the cities lay buried. Then, in the last years of the 16th century, the Spanish Viceroy ordered the construction of a conduit to carry a subterranean canal from the river Sarno to Torre d'Annunziata, a village which had no water supply. The tunnel was driven through the hill called Civita which was immediately over Pompeii. By this time the city lay fifteen to twenty feet below the earth's surface and the conduit only grazed it here and there. But it ran straight over the Temple of Isis, the Forum and the Street of Tombs, and the workmen turned up marble fragments and coins of the Emperor Nero. These finds excited curiosity in academic circles and the architect Fontana discovered some inscriptions and frescoed walls. The first real excavations, however, were carried out in 1748 under Charles Bourbon and his queen, Maria Amelia Christine. In this year the disinterment of Herculaneum was begun and a little later, in 1750–53, a large villa was discovered with a fine pillared peristyle and a bathing pool. Between the columns stood a perfect gallery of Greek and Roman sculpture, thirteen bronze statues and forty-seven busts. There were stately living-rooms adorned with frescoes, loggias, verandahs and a library lined with charred wooden cupboards full of papyrus rolls. But the excavation of Herculaneum presented numerous difficulties and the work was abandoned in favour of the far easier task of unearthing Pompeii.

Workmen who were building on the hill of Civita had come upon the vestiges of a wall. There were rumours that Pompeii lay buried there and the King gave the order for excavation work to be started on 23 March 1748. Almost immediately a splendid fresco of fruit, flowers and vine-leaves, part of the decoration of a dining-room, was discovered, together with a Roman helmet and pretty oil lamps in the form of open-mouthed heads. On 19 April the first of the dead was found, a man, from whose hands had fallen gold and silver coins of the time of Nero and Vespasian. Fresh, enchanting objects continually turned up: jewels, pottery groups, exquisitely designed kitchen and table ware and the charred contents of larders in beautiful dishes. But it was not until 1763 that it was indisputably proved that it was Pompeii which was being disinterred. On 16 August of that year the marble statue of a man in a toga was dug up; the pedestal bore an inscription referring to the Pompeians and showing that it had been erected at Pompeii.

The moving principles behind the work done at this time were greed and curiosity; it went on without method, spasmodically and with complete reliance on chance. Frescoes were cut out as soon as they were found and together with all the other objects found were taken to the King at Portici. Houses, courtyards and gardens were ruthlessly pillaged and despoiled. It was a quest not so much for the past as for treasure.

After the expulsion of the Bourbons the excavations were briefly under the directorship of Alexandre Dumas, who met with much local opposition and was unable to forward the work. Under Victor Emmanuele II the whole site was put in the charge of the gifted archaeologist Giuseppe Fiorelli and from that time (1860) the work was systematized. Fiorelli was the first to leave frescoes and statues where they were found, at the same time protecting them from exposure to the light and weather. The greater part of Herculaneum still awaits discovery beneath the town of Resina and till the modern houses can be shifted precious treasures, rich gardens and villas, temples, baths, frescoes and statues, little shops and taverns lie locked away in the hard tufa. But much has come to light in the present century. Excavation was carried on continually under the late Professor Maiuri, who employed modern drills and mechanical shovels to attack the hardened lava and revealed houses more elegant and larger than those of Pompeii, less regular in plan and adorned with finer frescoes and stucco work of a more refined character and with exquisite mosaics. In a servant's room of one of these houses in the winter of 1959 a prie-dieu, with an indentation above it in the form of a Christian cross, came to light. The cross that was fixed in the hollow may have been snatched away by its owner when he fled. It seems to point to the presence of secret followers of the Christian teaching in Herculaneum even at this exceptionally early date. It was the first sign of the power which was to transform ancient art and the ancient world.

Notes on the Plates

7

PAESTUM

TEMPLE OF

POSEIDON

Posidonia was one of the Greek colonies formed by the Achaeans from the north-west Peloponnese. It may have been founded from Sybaris, the city famed for the luxurious habits of its citizens and for its utter destruction by the Crotons in 510 BC. From the evidence of Corinthian pottery excavated at Paestum the colony seems to have originated in the late 7th century BC. Three great Doric temples still stand in a flat, melancholy waste between sea and toppling crags. The masonry is of the local stone, a deep orange colour, stained with grey lichen, cracked and weed-grown. The 'Temple of Poseidon' (still called by the name although it is now known to have been dedicated to Hera) dates from the middle of the 5th century BC. The cella is divided into three aisles by two rows of columns with smaller columns above; of these three remain on the north side and five on the south side. This is the only existing Greek temple with internal colonnades surmounted by smaller Doric columns. (See also page 32.) Only a century after the temple was built Posidonia fell into the hands of the Lucanians and in 273 BC it was taken by the Romans. The town gradually became depopulated chiefly owing to malaria, and was destroyed by the Saracens in 871.

8

AGRIGENTO, SICILY

TEMPLE OF

CASTOR AND

POLLUX

Less of this elegant temple has survived than of many of the Greek remains in Agrigento (Akragas), where the Temple of Concord is the best preserved of all Greek temples except for the Thesion in Athens. But this fragment is of special interest. The milky stucco with which the builders coated the local stone can still be seen clinging to the upper parts of the columns and to the architrave, and some of the stone slates with which the temple was roofed are still in place. The soffit of the cornice, in shadow in the photograph, is adorned with a painted design, a flowing stem and sprouting leaves in clear red and white, with a carved rosette at the corner. The temple dates from the 5th century BC. According to a local authority, Professor Arance, the name by which it is known is purely arbitrary and it was in reality dedicated to Dionysus Zagreus; both in proportion and ornament it resembles the Temple of Dionysus at Rhodes and like that building it is orientated towards the winter solstice.

Akragas was founded from Gela, some forty miles away, by Rhodian settlers there. The date usually given for the foundation is 580 BC, though from the evidence of pottery finds and the character of a shrine of Persephone outside the town walls (see page 33) the Greeks were in the district long before that date. Akragas reached the zenith of its fortunes in the 5th century when it wholly eclipsed its mother city and became one of the most important of all the Greek colonies in the west. It was the birthplace of Empedokles, the philosopher, who is said to have retired towards the end of his life to Etna where, from a hill still known as Torre de Filosofo, he spent his last years observing the activity of the volcano. With the disappearance of almost all of his writings the first record of eruptive phenomena made by a truly scientific mind was lost.

It was beside the Temple of Castor and Pollux that the Phoenicians encamped when under the formidable Hannibal they laid siege to the town, already under Roman rule in 261 BC; and it was in the ravine below the temple, watered by the Hypsas, that the siege began. Akragas fell for the second time in her history to her ancient enemy, the first time having been in 406 BC. The cypress trees mark the site of a Greek fishpond, now a watering place for animals. The whole terrain between the high ridge on which the temple stands and the town was part of the ancient colony and countless fragments of Greek pottery lying under the olive trees, and continually turned up by the plough, testify to its former presence. This intervening area is crossed by a rutted track, grooved for the passage of chariot wheels. It was the street leading in antiquity to the Gate of Heracleia. The modern town occupies the site of the Greek acropolis. The highest point, where the cathedral now stands, was the site of the Temple of Zeus Polieus.

The so-called 'Basilica', dating from the middle of the 6th century BC, is an extra-ordinarily primitive-looking structure. Less well preserved than the 'Temple of Poseidon', it is built of the same deep-toned travertine, though the material looks coarser and at close quarters is both more weather-beaten and more patterned with fossilized marine life. The *entasis* of the fluted shafts is so marked as to appear grotesque and the capitals project more widely than in any other Greek temple. The 'Basilica' has yet another peculiarity: it was divided internally by a central row of eight columns of which three remain. It may therefore have been dedicated to two deities. In the foreground of the photograph are seen two huge sacrificial altars; and beyond the temples are the remains of Lucanian and Roman houses, baths and public buildings.

9
PAESTUM
TEMPLE OF
POSEIDON AND
THE BASILICA

10
GIANT ATLAS
FIGURE
(*Temple of Zeus, Agrigento
Sicily*)

Not a single column of this vast Doric temple remains entire. One or two truncated pillars still rest on their plinths; their companions lie where they were hurled by an earthquake, split blocks of stone and fragments of cylinders so great of girth that a man may stand comfortably within each of their flutes. The Temple rivalled in size that of the great sanctuary at Selinunte, the largest of all Greek temples.

It was built about 480 BC after the Phoenicians had been defeated at Himera. The fallen colossus is the sole survivor of a number of giant figures that once supported the outer screen walls of the temple. This feature of the 'Temple of Zeus' was unique in Greek architecture. The *telemone*, or giant Atlas figure, is constructed on such a scale that at close quarters his stone limbs are scarcely recognizable. The mortar has long since crumbled from the joints in the masonry composing the ponderous torso and great thighs. But for the traces of expressive modelling in the shoulders and arms raised to support a mighty load, this figure might almost be taken for a freak of nature. The features are so ground down by exposure to the weather that the impression is of a ravaged, sunken mask reflected in wind-ruffled water.

Since this photograph was taken the *telemone* has been removed to the local museum and has been replaced by a plaster cast. (See also page 33.)

11
SYRACUSE, SICILY
GREEK THEATRE
AT EPIPOLAE

Constructed at the beginning of the 5th century BC, the theatre was rebuilt under Hieron II during the 3rd century. Hewn out of the solid rock and divided into nine sectors, it is one of the largest of Greek theatres. It is situated on the bare, bleached upland called Epipolae by the Greeks because, as Thucydides said, 'this place is higher than the town'. Aeschylus supervised a performance of the *Persae* here in 472 BC. Tidied, thoroughly excavated, divested of every weed, and guarded by a uniformed attendant who hastens to expostulate if so much as an orange is consumed within his sight, and who would certainly have prevented Brydon from eating the cold fowl he was so thankful to have brought with him in 1761, the worn semicircle of tiered seats and narrow flights of steps – utterly exposed, sun-soaked, overrun with lizards and black snakes – is yet intensely moving. It presents a significant contrast to the town with its featureless modern suburbs and hideous sprawl of industry stretched out below. The clamour rises, but close at hand the only sound is the plash of water coming from the *nymphaeum* above the theatre. Around the larger of the two *praecinctiones* runs a frieze bearing the names of Hieron II, his queens Philistis and Nereis, and Zeus Olympios in large Greek characters.

12
TAORMINA, SICILY
THEATRE

Tauromenion was established as a Greek colony in the 5th century BC but Greeks are known to have been here already in the 8th century: according to Thucydides they first landed at nearby Naxos in 734. The theatre was built in the Hellenistic period and almost entirely rebuilt by the Romans during the 2nd century BC, a circumstance visually most fortunate, for nothing could more perfectly harmonize with the brilliant romantic landscape than the deep pink bricks and luxuriant Corinthian capitals of the Roman structure. It is a fabled scene that unfolds from this high spot, with Mount Etna in the background. Along the shore, to the left of the column in the foreground, are the jagged rocks hurled by the blinded Polyphemus at Odysseus and his companions. Close by is the sandy cove where the Greeks first disembarked. Among the hills shelving down to the Ionian sea Apollo's flocks are said to have grazed, and there runs the 'fiume freddo', the river celebrated in the legend of Acis and Galatea. It was there that Acis was supposed to have been slain by Polyphemus and changed by the compassionate gods into a river. (See also page 35.)

This is one of thirty-three reliefs recovered from the site of a Doric temple which lies about five and a half miles farther along the coast from the Temple of Demeter. It is now in the Museum at Paestum. It dates from the early 6th century BC and the provincial style is seen at once to have something in common with Athenian work of the same period – the archaic Korai, for instance, from the ancient temple of Athene in the Acropolis Museum. But these figures are less idealized, less taut, more stocky, more crudely earthy and, curiously enough, more realistic than contemporary sculpture in Greece.

13
PAESTUM, SICILY
SANCTUARY OF
HERA ARGIVA:
METOPE RELIEF

Dedicated to St Lucy, a native of Syracuse who suffered martyrdom under Galerius, the cathedral was built during the 7th century from the ruins of the great Doric temple of Athene of the 5th century BC. Nearly all the incrustations of later ages have been removed from the noble interior, which incorporates the greater part of Athene's shrine. The photograph shows the south aisle with side chapels leading off between the Doric columns through wrought iron gates, some of which are of Saracenic workmanship. Syracuse was under Saracen domination from 878 until 1085, when it fell to the Normans. The city was originally founded by the Corinthians in the 8th century BC and became the richest of the Greek colonies in Sicily. (See also page 34.)

14
SYRACUSE, SICILY
CATHEDRAL

The amphitheatre lies outside and below the town of Sutri (see page 36). It is small and elliptical, cut from the dark red rock and overhung with great ilex trees and by a blasted evergreen oak. The corridors, seats and vomitories and the flights of steps are in many parts perfect, although dripping with moisture and stained with grey-green moss and lichen. The amphitheatre is thought to date from about the 1st century BC when Sutri, repeatedly captured and lost again, was under Roman rule. Some authorities

15
SUTRI
ETRUSCAN
AMPHITHEATRE

have ascribed this theatre to the Romans, but the method of construction, carved rather than built, is peculiarly Etruscan and the details, such as the narrowing of the doors towards the top, correspond to those found in Etruscan rock-cut tombs. The doors in the podium open into a vaulted corridor which surrounds the arena, a very rare arrangement. There is also a broad corridor running round the upper edge of the structure and above it, on one side, in a wall of rock thickly overgrown with ivy and saplings, slender half columns can be made out, carved in relief with a cornice above. Perhaps statues of the gods in whose honour the games were held once stood between these columns. In the same wall there are several niches of a sepulchral character which may have been the work of early Christians.

The Sutri amphitheatre was hidden for centuries beneath a forest of holm oaks and ilex trees; it was first excavated by the Marquis Savorelli at the end of the last century. He erected a balustrade belvedere in his garden on the cliff above the amphitheatre, from which he could look down on his discovery. It is still there.

16
ETRUSCAN WINGED
HORSES IN
TERRACOTTA
(*Palazzo Vitelleschi, Tarquinia*)

These horses date from the 3rd century BC. They are about 3 ft 9 ins high and about 4 feet long and were harnessed to the chariot of a god that decorated the pediment of a temple on the Ara della Regina, a spot on the Piano de Civita, the site of the Etruscan town, still called Tarchuna. It is a high bare tableland divided by a ravine from the modern town of Tarquinia which adjoins the necropolis of its Etruscan predecessor. There is now no sign of life on this desolate, tree-less stretch, yet it was obviously the site of a city, for the most casual inspection reveals brick-bats, fragments of earthenware and pieces of worked stone and marble everywhere underfoot. The Ara della Regina is on the highest part of the plateau and appears to have been the site of several temples.

The Etruscans were renowned for their work in terracotta, especially for work on a large scale. Whereas much of their architecture resembled carving rather than building, they showed a marked preference in their plastic work for modelling rather than carving. Clay and bronze were more suited to the expression of their bold, personal vision than stone. Their astonishing work in these materials exercised a profound influence on the arts of the Christian era in Italy (see pages 97, 102, 111, 151–2).

17
ETRUSCAN
NOBLEMAN
(*Palazzo Vitelleschi, Tarquinia*)

This reclining stone-carved figure on the lid of his sarcophagus dates from the late 4th or early 3rd century BC. It was the custom of the Etruscans to commemorate the deceased resting on their stone couches not in the attitude of sleep or death, which was to characterize medieval sepulchral effigies, but half sitting up as at a banquet. Married couples usually sit side by side on the same sarcophagus lid and together they await the eternal banquet of another world. This isolated figure whose pillows are flanked by a sphinx and by a round-faced, dog-like lion very much like those which lie at the feet of knights on Gothic tombs, is not depicted at a banquet. He lies in a more recumbent position and holds in one hand a shallow bowl, the *patera*, with an obol in it for entry fee to the underworld.

The sarcophagus on whose lid this figure rests dates from the late 4th century BC and the name of the deceased is Ramtha Apatrui. She is wearing a typical Etruscan small round hat and a large ring on the fourth finger of her left hand, the finger most favoured by the Greeks and Romans also. The reason for the preference is said to be that the Egyptians had discovered by dissection that a certain nerve led from the fourth finger to the heart and thus this digit was singled out for distinction. The Etruscans were passionately fond of jewellery, which was remarkable for its technical accomplishment.

While the lids of Etruscan sarcophagi were made expressly for the individual whose remains they enclose, the sarcophagi themselves were probably manufactured wholesale by the Etruscan undertakers. The figure of the deceased was sometimes modelled in the lifetime of the subject and sometimes made after death from a small terracotta head taken from life, such as have been found in large numbers in Etruscan tombs. The figure of this woman shows traces of colouring and the eyeballs were probably enamelled originally. The outstanding naturalism and vivid characterization of the Etruscan effigies were important influences on the later Roman art of portraiture.

18
ETRUSCAN FIGURE
IN TERRACOTTA
(*Palazzo Vitelleschi, Tarquinia*)

The arch at Benevento dates from AD 114 and is the most elaborately decorated of all Roman triumphal arches. It has a single opening and the marble reliefs depict the story of Trajan's life, testify to his popularity with soldiers and civilians alike, and commemorate his military virtues. The central relief in the coffered vault shows a winged Victory crowning Trajan with laurels in a haphazard border of trophies of arms, such as occurs in the work of Palladio at Vicenza. The egg and dart ornament and the rosettes in the centres of the coffers are carved with marvellous delicacy and precision.

19, 21
BENEVENTO
ARCH OF TRAJAN:
RELIEF AND
COFFERED VAULT

The splendid Arch of Septimius Severus, built entirely of marble and surviving almost unscathed, was one of the latest monuments to be added to the Forum Romanorum. It was dedicated by the people and the senate to the Emperor and his sons Caracalla and Geta in AD 203 on the occasion of the tenth anniversary of Septimius Severus's accession to the throne, and commemorated his Parthian victories. The summit of the arch was once adorned with statues of the Emperor and his two sons in a quadriga with soldiers on either side. During the Middle Ages the arch was surmounted by two towers, one of which was used as the campanile of the church of SS. Sergius and Bacchus. In

20
ROME
ARCH OF
SEPTIMIUS
SEVERUS,
AND FORUM
ROMANORUM

the mid-18th century the side arches were walled in and let as shops. The reliefs illustrate Severus's victories in the east.

Through the central opening, at the highest point along the Via Sacra, the oldest and most important road in the Forum, can be seen the Arch of Titus, built in AD 81 by Domitian to celebrate the destruction of Jerusalem by his father Vespasian and his brother Titus. The arch is cased in marble and decorated with reliefs showing the Romans removing precious booty from the temple of Jerusalem, the triumphal procession with the captive Jews and the apotheosis of Titus.

In the earliest days of Rome the Forum was an uninhabited swamp, but as the town spread the marsh was drained and became in time the centre of public life. It reached the height of its splendour during the imperial period. The first sign of decay was when building operations came to a sudden halt after Constantine's departure. Sheer neglect, the inability of the municipal authorities to maintain the regular cleaning services as the population of Rome declined, played as large a part as pillage and wanton destruction in the ruination of the Forum. Dust gathered and was changed by the rain into mud upon which coarse grass began to sprout; filth and rubbish accumulated and the level of the deposit rose steadily until a deep layer of soil concealed the Forum. It became a pastoral waste where cattle grazed, giving it the name by which it was still known during the 19th century, *Campo Vaccino*. A wooded path ran from the Arch of Septimius Severus to the Arch of Titus and the remains of antiquity rose from copses and flower-sprinkled turf. The systematic rehabilitation of the Forum began in earnest in the second half of the last century. The vaults of ancient arches, the shattered walls of baths and temples, fallen columns and broken temples were slowly brought to light and restored. Ancient Rome returned, a dead, gaunt, pitifully stripped relic of its mighty past.

Today, though shaken by traffic and overrun by thousands of tourists, the Forum is visually more romantic. In early spring when the whole expanse is vested in tender green, sweet-smelling fennel, ground ivy and an occasional myrtle bush, permitted to take root in a block of masonry too amorphous to be recognized and restored, it is still possible to recapture something of the impressions of William Beckford when he stood in the Forum in 1783 and to savour with Henry James's Winterbourne the delicious and mysterious mingling of the freshness of the year with the antiquity of the battered monuments.

22, 23
ROME
THE PANTHEON
AND ITS PORTICO

This great circular building with its immense, shallow dome is the most completely preserved of the monuments of ancient Rome. The diameter of the cupola, 142½ feet internally, has only been surpassed in our own day by the huge span of some of Nervi's concrete domes. The Roman masterpiece is not, however, of concrete, but of brickwork and thick mortar laid in horizontal courses. The circular wall is of concrete 20 feet thick faced externally with brick banded with layers of tiles; the brick is part of the structure, as can be seen by the relieving arches. At the time of Hadrian the lower storey of the Pantheon was faced externally with large slabs of gleaming Pentelic marble and the upper storeys were coated with stucco. The dome, including the stepped, lower part, was sheathed in gilded bronze plates which were removed to Constantinople in AD 655 and replaced by lead. The building is lit by a single unglazed opening like a great eye in the crown of the dome which still retains its original circular bronze cornice.

A Latin inscription on the portico records that the first building of 27 BC was the work of Agrippa: M. AGRIPPA L.F. CONSUL TERTIUM FECIT. The rotunda stood to the south of a nymphaeum for plants and running water and the portico faced south. The Pantheon was destroyed by fire during the reign of Titus and rebuilt by Trajan. Shortly afterwards it was struck by lightning and restored by Hadrian, who transferred the rotunda to the site of the nymphaeum, re-erecting Agrippa's portico at a higher level, facing north now instead of south. The Temple was extensively restored in AD 202 by Septimius Severus and Caracalla.

The Pantheon was dedicated to the gods of the seven planets: Apollo, Diana, Mercury, Venus, Mars, Jupiter and Saturn. In 609 it was consecrated by Pope Boniface IV as a place of Christian worship. Pope Urban VIII Barberini used bronze from the ornaments of the coffers inside the dome to cast the columns for the Baldacchino in St Peter's.

The Corinthian portico forms a majestic entrance to this grandest of circular temples. The plain columns, forming a triple colonnade, are of marble and granite with luxuriant capitals of white Pentelic marble. At the back of the portico, on either side of the huge bronze doors which were once plated with gold, are niches in which stood colossal statues of Agrippa and Augustus.

The marble elephant in the Piazza della Minerva, seen in the foreground of plate 22, was designed by Bernini and bears on its back a little Egyptian obelisk of the 6th century BC discovered in the ruins of the Temple of Isis in this district.

One of the most striking features of this remarkable building is the series of arcades encircling the amphitheatre and forming covered ambulatories (plate 24).

The Colosseum was begun by Vespasian in AD 70 and completed by Domitian in AD 82, except for the upper storey which was added in the 3rd century. With its three tiers, it held about 80,000 spectators. The building rose on the site of the artificial lake in Nero's palace garden and owed its name to a neighbouring monument, a giant statue of Nero carved by the sculptor Zenodorus. After Nero's death, Vespasian changed it into a statue of the Sun with a head surrounded by rays. Hadrian had it moved to another part of Rome and later it disappeared. But its memory survived and the Flavian

24, 25
ROME
COLOSSEUM OR
FLAVIAN
AMPHITHEATRE

Amphitheatre has been known throughout the centuries not by its true name but by that of the lost monument.

The whole gigantic edifice was built up without the support which the Greeks and Etruscans had secured for their buildings by carving the auditorium out of the earth (see plates 11, 12 and 15); and the feat was made possible by the use of concrete. The building is of exceptional interest today when architects are using similar synthetic materials on a vast scale to create, as the Romans did, a universal style that overrides the limitations of local conditions. The concrete used for the Colosseum varied according to the purpose for which it was required. Thus it was mixed with lava for the solid foundations, with tufa and brick for the supporting walls, (which is the source of the splendid russet colour of all those parts that have lost their marble casing) and with pumice stone for the vaulting to reduce its weight. The massive piers supporting the arcades were originally covered with marble held in place by metal clamps, the holes for which can be seen in the concrete.

The clear composition of this great work is perhaps even more impressive in its ruined state than when it stood entire. Its stupendous proportions and complex structure are ordered by the constant repetition of arch and attached column and by the sweeping lines of the unbroken entablatures round the oval building. The decorative columns are of three orders, Tuscan, Ionic and Corinthian. The arches of the two upper storeys were originally filled with statues.

The sumptuous shows with which the opening of the Colosseum was celebrated under Titus, before it was completed, lasted for one hundred days; and on this occasion included the re-enactment of the story of the pirate Lareolus who had been crucified after a lifetime of violence and sacrilege. The actor who took the part was actually nailed to the cross and an infuriated bear was let loose on him. The horrifying sight is described by Martial as a wonderfully entertaining spectacle. Mortal combats and dramatic hunts were daily part of the programme. In addition to such scenes of bloodshed there were also naval exhibitions in the Colosseum and pipes for flooding the arena still exist.

The Emperor Honorius prohibited gladiatorial combats and by the 6th century wild animals were no longer let loose on one another. During the Middle Ages the building was used as a fortress and in the course of the 15th, 16th and 17th centuries the ruins were plundered to provide building material for churches and palaces. It was only when Pope Benedict XIV consecrated the Colosseum to the memory of all the Christian martyrs who had died in the arena that the structure was spared further depredation.

Beyond the Colosseum (in plate 25) can be seen the Arch of Constantine, built in AD 312 to commemorate this emperor's victory over Maxentius. It celebrates the famous battle in which Constantine's soldiers bore the monogram of Christ on their shields and saw the sign of the Cross in the sky.

This arch, like that of Septimius Severus, was once surmounted by a quadriga. It is adorned with reliefs, mostly taken from other monuments, showing scenes from the lives of Trajan, Hadrian and Marcus Aurelius.

Known also as the Basilica of Constantine, this great building was begun by Maxentius in AD 308 and completed by Constantine in 313. It is adjacent to the Forum. The Roman basilicas were halls of justice and commercial exchanges. Architecturally they form a conspicuous link between classic and Christian building for they served the early Christians as models for their churches. The striking feature of this, the most magnificent basilica that ever stood in Rome, was the enormous span of the vaults that roofed not only the central nave but both the north and south aisles. This view shows part of the vaults of the northern aisle with their deep brick coffering. The basilica is carried out entirely in brick and the massive ruins are of a glowing dark red colour. The roof was originally covered with gilded bronze plates which were removed in 626 by Honorius I for the decoration of St Peter's. In the main apse was enthroned a colossal statue of Constantine, the head of which now lies in the courtyard of the Palazzo dei Conservatori. One of the Corinthian columns from the Basilica was set up by Paul V in the piazza of S. Maria Maggiore.

The top of the campanile seen through the arch belongs to the church of S. Francesca Romana, built on the site of a Temple of Venus erected by Hadrian. The belfry dates from the 12th century.

26
ROME
BASILICA OF
MAXENTIUS:
VAULT

Formerly known as the Pons Aemilius, it was begun in 179 BC by M. Aemilius Lepidus and Marcus Fulvius Nobilior and finished in 142 BC by P. Scipio Africanus and L. Mummius. The martyr brothers Simplicius and Faustinus were thrown from this bridge into the Tiber in the time of Diocletian. The oldest of the Tiber stone bridges, it was three times heavily restored under different Popes before the inundation of 1598 carried away two of its three arches.

27
ROME
PONTE ROTTO

The Forum, seen here from the north through the Triumphal Arch of Germanicus, was the centre of the life of the city and these desolate ruins were once filled with a bustling throng. Wheeled traffic was not permitted in the Forum and on certain occasions it was completely cut off by means of gates and grills. The stone bollards in front of the arch were placed there as obstructions to vehicles. Following the severe earthquake of AD 62, the public buildings were restored but the forty statues, some of them equestrian, which had adorned the Forum were not replaced.

28
POMPEII
FORUM

The great rectangular piazza of the Forum lies to the right of the arch. The building immediately to the left inside the arch is the ruined Marcellum or covered market of Augustan date. It was a large square space surrounded with porticos in which were shops. In the centre was a circular construction with a domed roof and a water tank which was connected by an underground channel to the sewers. It was here that the fishmongers washed and scraped their merchandise. A quantity of fish-scales were found in the tank when it was cleared. The remaining columns are of white Carrara marble.

The imposing ruins at the farther end of the street belong to the Building of Eumachia. An inscription in large letters on a marble tablet over the side entrance in Via dell'Abbondanza records that the edifice was dedicated by the priestess Eumachia, patroness of the corporation of fullers to the Concordia Augustus and to Pietas, personifications of Livia, wife of Augustus. The fullers (cloth-makers and dyers) were the most active and important group of workers in Pompeii, and these were their guild premises. They combined storehouses, meeting halls and work-rooms and even perhaps lodgings for travellers. The façade towards the Forum boasts a double row of marble columns, and a wide marble portal with a beautiful spiral decoration of acanthus leaves leads into a huge court surrounded by a two-storeyed colonnade.

29
POMPEII
VIA STABIANA

The Via Stabiana, seen here from the Via dell'Abbondanza looking towards the Porta di Stabiae, is a characteristic Pompeian street. It has a raised footpath and, in the foreground, stepping-stones placed across the thoroughfare at its junction with Via dell'Abbondanza for the use of pedestrians. This district, belonging to the first Augustan period, was one of the last to be developed in Pompeii before the catastrophe (see page 39), although the gateway is probably the oldest in the town. The Via Stabiana was one of the main arteries of Pompeii leading to the neighbouring port. The excellent preservation of the streets of the city clearly shows the way in which the various quarters were divided. Laid out in rectangles bounded by main roads and crossed by minor streets and alleys, the plan resembled the modern grid system as opposed to the haphazard growth of the medieval town. On the left of the Via Stabiana are the ruins of shops; on the right, the small covered theatre used for musical recitals and mimes.

30
HERCULANEUM
HOUSE OF
NEPTUNE AND
AMPHITRITE:
ATRIUM

The rich decoration consists of marble masks and brilliant mosaics, the predominating colour of which is an intense cerulean blue. Whereas at Pompeii wall mosaics are mostly confined to niches and fountains, elaborate wall mosaics are a feature of many of the Herculaneum houses so far disinterred. This house is named after the subject of a huge mosaic on the back wall of the courtyard. In the foreground, part of a pool is seen with a beautiful fountain. Unlike most of the Pompeian houses this dwelling is two-storeyed.

The little picture of the Rape of Europa shown in plate 31 adorns a modest artisan's house and shows the type of decoration found in even the most humble homes of Pompeii and Herculaneum. Plate 32 shows a detail from the painted frieze in the trichinium of the House of the Vettii. Excavated towards the end of the last century, this is one of the most luxurious houses in Pompeii, with splendid murals and a charmingly laid-out garden. It was the home of two rich merchants who bore the same nomen and praenomen, Aulus Vettius Restitus and Aulus Vettius Conviva. The house stands in the Strada di Mercurio between the Vico del Labirinto and the Vico degli Scienziati. The murals are among the best preserved and most elaborate in the city and belong to the latest, almost purely ornamental style of Pompeian painting, of the period from the time of Claudius to AD 79. The frieze from which this detail is taken shows *amorini* engaged in various arts and occupations of daily life.

31, 32
HERCULANEUM
MURAL PAINTINGS

The paintings at Pompeii and Herculaneum are not true frescoes. They were done in tempera with an emulsion of hydrated and saponified lime as the binding medium. The extreme brilliance of the colours seems to be the result of wax varnish and repeated polishing with a soft cloth. Many samples of raw pigments have been found in houses at Pompeii and Herculaneum which were still being decorated at the time of the catastrophe. They show that artists were in the habit of using an elaborate palette. The most popular pigments appear to have been minium and cinnabar (which when mixed with rubica, ochre and sinoper provided the various tints of the famous 'Pompeian red'), caerulum blue, purple, green extracted from a copper silicate, yellow, black of two shades, and white made of several varieties of chalk.

Easel pictures were popular, painted on wooden panels, prepared like the walls with a ground of fine plaster compounded of marble dust. Few of these panels have survived.

Only partially excavated as yet, the Basilica, near the Forum, is decorated on the concave surfaces of niches giving on to the interior of the great hall with paintings illustrating episodes from classical mythology. This one is now in the Museo Nazionale, Naples. They were the work of a painter of the early Flavian period whose aim was solidity and realistic modelling. Maiuri suggests that the painter was not a native of Herculaneum but probably came from near-by Neapolis. If this was so, it enhances the strangeness of the resemblance of these murals to the work of Neapolitan artists painting fifteen hundred years later, artists such as Mattia Preti, Andrea Vaccaro, Giovanni Battista Caracciolo and Luca Giordano.

33
CHIRON
INSTRUCTING
ACHILLES
(*Formerly in the Basilica,
Herculaneum*)

The excavation of the great thoroughfare running from the Forum to the Porta di Sarno, Pompeii was only begun in 1911–12 and was completed under Professor Maiuri between 1951 and 1954. This street was the heart of the most commercial quarter of the

34
POMPEII VIA
DELL'ABBONDANZA

prosperous, busy city. During the excavations attention was concentrated on the disinterment of the fronts of the shops and houses. Several of the dwellings in the Via dell'Abbondanza boast an upper floor and in some cases balconies overlook the street. More than anywhere else in Pompeii this street is haunted by the sense of the life which was so abruptly extinguished by the great eruption of Vesuvius in AD 79. Election notices are painted up on the walls in neat red letters, the heavy doorway of a dyer's and cleaner's stands ajar, and shop signs mark the entrance to the workrooms of a cloth-maker, M. Vecilius Verecundus. One house is in process of being redecorated and the heap of chalk fragments from which the plaster was prepared still lies on the floor. There is a bar for hot and cold drinks where the terracotta and bronze vessels, the hanging lamps and the petty cash were all found in place; exotic female names are scrawled on the outside wall of this establishment, Aegle, Maria, Smyrna, together with the nickname Asellino, damsels who perhaps served in the bar and in the inn above it. Farther along the street is the painted sign of another tavern, a still life of amphorae and metal mugs with gold reflections.

35
POMPEIAN STRUCK
DOWN IN FLIGHT
(*Antiquarium, Pompeii*)

The idea of making casts of all the victims found at Pompeii was conceived by the archaeologist Giuseppe Fiorelli who took charge of the excavations at Pompeii and Herculaneum in 1860. The ashes in which the dead lay solidified while the bodies were still intact, thus preserving an exact mould of those bodies after they themselves had dwindled to skeletons. Fiorelli filled the moulds with plaster of Paris and thus obtained casts of the dead people which reproduced the shape and position of their limbs and even the expressions on their faces with the most moving verisimilitude.

36–40
ARTICLES FOUND
AT POMPEII AND
HERCULANEUM

36. Bread found in the shop belonging to the baker Modestus, off the Vico Storto, not far from the Forum.

37. Silver strainer.

38. Glass oil flask in the shape of a mallet.

39. Clay vessels with traces of wine in the bottom, found in a tavern. It is inscribed with the name Anogoni. The amphorae in this tavern were kept on wooden shelves.

40. Eggs, walnuts, lentils and carobs in the dishes in which they were discovered on the tables of the triclinium in the priests' lodgings of the Temple of Isis, Pompeii. The priests had just begun their meal when the eruption took them by surprise.

The villa dates from the 3rd or early 4th century AD and is especially interesting for its wealth of floor mosaics. It is a large, most luxurious villa in enchanting surroundings, a shallow fertile valley watered by the Gela. A horseshoe-shaped courtyard, enclosed by Corinthian columns, magnificent reception rooms, a three-apsed dining-room, a library, bathrooms and innumerable small private chambers have been skilfully adapted to the sloping ground. The walls have crumbled away but the character of each room is exhibited by the wonderfully fresh floor mosaics. Nothing is known of the builder and owner of this great villa. He must have been some luxury-loving Roman who chose to reside in Sicily, perhaps when Constantine transferred the seat of the Empire to Byzantium. The mosaics are an indication of his wealth and his tastes. The subject matter of these mosaics is charged with mystery and probably has some esoteric significance. A large composition showing Orpheus and an apsidal image of a strange dusky sorceress-like Venus dominate the villa. A wide corridor stretching for many yards is completely taken up with scenes of the chase, featuring among the captives of the hunt a man in a gilded cage clutched by a tawny griffin of ferocious aspect. Watching the hunt, protected by two men holding shields, is an enigmatical priestly figure with a grave expression, wearing a long robe and a richly coloured cloak decorated with oriental designs. It has been suggested that this hunting scene is a symbolic depiction of the Christian paradise. Certainly the owner of the villa could scarcely have remained aloof from the new religion, for the Sicilian saints Agata, Lucia and Nympha must all have been martyred either just before or during the building of this rural retreat. But what are we to deduce from the attitude of a man whose bathroom was adorned with bikini-clad girls vivaciously disporting themselves not only with discus, dumb-bells and parasol, but with crowns and palms, the emblems of St Agata?

41
PIAZZA ARMERINA,
SICILY
MOSAIC FROM
ROMAN VILLA

Hadrian's immense, sprawling villa, almost the size of a town with its libraries, small baths, great baths, Marine Theatre, stadium, swimming pools, Philosopher's Hall, courtyards and colonnades, is a monument to his passion for touring the Empire. He named the various buildings and their landscape setting after places in Greece and Egypt which had given him particular pleasure: the Lyceum, the Academia, the Prytaneum and the Stoa Poikile at Athens, the Vale of Tempe in Thessaly and the Canopus, a famous Alexandrian canal leading to the temple of Serapis. The Emperor did not seek to reproduce these places, only to recall them to memory. The Canopus is the only part of the villa where the original name can be applied with certainty. For Hadrian the cult of Serapis, whose sanctuary stood at the end of the Canopus, was more than a whim. The oracle of Serapis had promised him a long life on condition that a youth died for him, and Antinous, the beautiful boy to whom the Emperor was devoted, is supposed to have offered his life as a sacrifice to his benefactor. In any case the youth

42
TIVOLI
VILLA OF
HADRIAN:
THE CANOPUS

was drowned in the Nile in mysterious circumstances and many statues of Antinous as a god, scattered about the villa, show the direction of Hadrian's thoughts and feelings. The Canopus has recently been restored almost to its original state. Judging from this, the great villa was far less stimulating to the eye and imagination when it was entire than during its long life as a ruin. The marble colonnade is exquisitely graceful, but the composition is marred by the odd assortment of sculpture round the edge of the water. The statues of Mars and an Amazon which appear in the photograph are reproductions of those found on the site and now in a small museum close to the Canopus. They are accompanied by copies of Greek caryatids, indifferent Roman pieces and by a stone crocodile that might have come straight out of Disneyland.

The villa was Hadrian's favourite residence and was built for him between AD 125 and 135. The exact details of its history after Hadrian's death are not known. It was plundered by the barbarian invaders and, although excavations were begun at the end of the 15th century under Alexander VI and have gone on ever since, the gigantic ruins were embowered in a romantic wilderness of creepers and wild flowers almost until the close of the Victorian era. The Villa was purchased by the Italian State in 1870 and systematically cleared from that time on.

43
ROME
PYRAMID OF
CAIUS CESTIUS

The Praetor Caius Cestius died in 12 BC. His monument near the Porta S. Paolo is of brick cased in dazzling white marble. The Protestant cemetery shown in the foreground, once remote and silent, now strewn with litter and shattered by the roar of heavy traffic, is a memorial to many northerners who sought fulfilment in Italy and died there. Among the graves are those of Shelley, Keats, Severn, Trelawney and Ballantyne, Alexander von Humboldt and Goethe's son. The shadow of this great pyramidal tomb fell upon St Paul when he walked out of Rome to his martyrdom.

Plates 7-43

1

21

31

32

34

35

6
8

37
39

Christian Italy

THE CHANGE FROM PAGANISM TO CHRISTIANITY was one of the greatest revolutions in the world's history, greater even perhaps than that which science and technology are effecting in our own day. And yet this readjustment of men's attitude to the universe was not accompanied by any startling innovations in the forms of art. A new direction of thought and feeling is certainly apparent in the Roman villa at Piazza Armerina (plate 41) but it is expressed in the mould deriving directly from the pagan world: there is no trace of Christian influence in the external features of this or of any of the works of the Roman Empire belonging to the Christian era which were illustrated in the previous section. Nor can any sharp dividing line be drawn stylistically between those works and the buildings, sculpture and decoration comprised in the present section. The development is rather that of a continuous and continually transformed tradition. The force of the impact of the dynamic contrast between Paganism and Christianity in Italy is heightened by the fact that the new gods owe so much to the old; the masterpieces of antiquity are the dominant source for all that came later. Again and again the basic forms and motifs are revived to embody totally different attitudes in totally different combinations while remaining recognizably the same.

Renaissance, Mannerist and Baroque art are obviously dependent on the antique. The connection between Byzantine, Romanesque and Gothic art and classical example is at first glance less apparent, but emerges with increasing clarity the more closely these arts are examined. The persistence in Early Christian and medieval architecture of Roman structural devices is generally recognized. A detailed account of this influence — it would inevitably have to include a discussion of the vexed question as to whether or not the Romans had already solved the problem of setting the circular base of a dome upon a square ground plan, as they had according to Rivoira (*Lombardic Architecture*) and E. H. Swift (*Roman Sources of Christian Art*) — would be out of place in this brief survey. Domed circular buildings were in any case common in the pagan world and their plans were soon exploited in the service of the new faith. S. Costanza, Rome (324–6) is but one instance of a church based directly on the cupola-crowned rotundas of the Romans, of which the most important surviving example is the Pantheon. The Etruscan and Roman system of vaulting was the basis of the waggon-vaults and intersecting vaults of Romanesque architecture and the source from which the most characteristic feature of Gothic art, the ribbed vault, was derived. And yet it was not on Italian soil but farther north that this development was to achieve its most sublime expression.

The Roman basilican plan, with its three aisles divided by columns, was adopted all over the Christian world and played an important part in the ritual arrangement of the church interior; but it was of special significance in Italy. Architects working there during the first two or three centuries of official Christianity and throughout the Middle Ages could not but be aware of the past around them. Many of the ancient monuments had been put to new uses. In Rome the Theatre of Marcellus, the Mausoleum of Augustus, the Colosseum, the Arches of Constantine and Trajan as well as the Baths of Trajan had all been turned into fortresses; the rites of the new religion were being celebrated in the Baths of Diocletian, in the Pantheon and in the basilicas. It is not surprising that in the Eternal City the ghosts of the dead Empire were never laid; and that of all the three hundred churches of Rome only one, S. Maria Sopra Minerva, exhibits the pointed arch. But it was not only in Rome that architects showed a fixed bias towards the basilican plan. The pyramidal façade with a marked horizontal emphasis was everywhere preferred and persisted throughout the centuries when architecture elsewhere in Europe was emphatically vertical; it proved itself the strongest element in those recombinations of mingled styles, the Roman, the Byzantine, Saracenic and Lombard, dictated by the varying influences in different parts of Italy of commerce, conquest and the presiding genius of place. The influence of classical models is betrayed by the construction of the Cathedral at Monreale, embroidered with Moorish arabesques and Byzantine mosaics and with Greek and Cufic lettering; of the brick interiors of S. Zeno, Verona and of Cremona Cathedral; of the severe and solemn Duomo at Orvieto (plate 67) with its striped pillars; of the Duomo of Pistoia embellished with green serpentine; and of the pallid stone sanctuaries of Bari, Trani, and Troia – though all these were so far apart geographically. Round arches, colonnades of pillars and pilasters, large rectangular spaces and a reliance on the design of the basilica are everywhere in evidence.

Even when a centralized plan was adopted, the idea of a three-aisled rectilinear structure was never quite lost sight of and was frequently combined with a cruciform upper structure as at S. Mark's, Venice. And even at S. Vitale, Ravenna, where the geometry of cylinders and prisms piled against an octagon makes an impression of strong verticality, and angular, complex vistas create an atmosphere of restlessness, these are offset by the longitudinal sanctuary. And this, the major building in the West of Justinian's period, is unique in Italy. S. Apollinare in Classe, erected by Justinian on the site of a temple of Apollo, and S. Apollinare Novo, built by Theodoric the Great in 493, the two Christian churches at Ravenna roughly contemporary with S. Vitale, are undisguised basilicas although they were in all probability the work of Byzantine craftsmen.

The exterior of S. Vitale, though so much restored that the fabric now looks unpleasantly mechanical, displays large thin bricks with conspicuous mortar joints very much like Roman brickwork. The Roman predilection for this material was the origin of a tradition of brick building in Italy which in other European countries lapsed almost completely between the time of the Roman occupation and the late Middle Ages. Even where stone was scarce it was considered the only worthy material for important secular and ecclesiastical architecture. It is therefore astonishing to find an uninterrupted use of brick in Italy and to come, behind ornate façades like those of the Cathedrals of Parma or Crema, upon austere walls of brick indistinguishable from those of the Pantheon or of Hadrian's Villa. Brick forms the fabric of the noble Cathedrals of Modena, Ferrara and Fidenza; and of San Petronio and of the group of buildings comprising Santo Stefano, Bologna; of San Nicolo, Treviso, the Palazzo Comunale, Siena and the Palazzo dei Tribunale, Piacenza, among innumerable other examples. Frequently brick is combined with terracotta ornament, the use of which had been so highly developed by the Etruscans. The Duomo, Cremona; S. Francesco, Piacenza; S. Pietro, Castelarquoto; S. Marco and the Palazzo Casa Borromeo, Milan; S. Maria Del Carmine, Pavia; the churches of Spirito Santo and S. Giacomo and the Palazzo Comunale, Bologna; and the Palazzo Borgheresi, San Gimignano, are but a few of the many medieval brick buildings in Italy enriched in this way. Local materials were more widely used in the Romanesque and Gothic periods than they had been in Roman times and it was therefore chiefly in northern Italy, where there was little stone, that brick was extensively cultivated. In the south churches were built of the stone of the district, but even here brick sometimes occurred. The little church of La Cattolica, Stilo, in Calabria, is constructed wholly of this material and S. Maria d'Aracoeli raises a façade of plain brick above the marble buildings of the Capitol in Rome.

If the early use of brick in Italy seems singular to anyone accustomed to northern versions of the Romanesque and Gothic styles, the innate affinity of Italian craftsmen and architects with the art of classical antiquity was responsible for many other features which either never occur at all or are extremely rare in the rest of Europe. First of all there is the invariable custom of regarding the campanile as separate from the main body of a church. In northern countries it is incorporated in the building as the most aspiring member of an upward-soaring whole. In Italy the campanile usually stands alone, reserved for its original purpose of housing the bells, and emphasizing by way of contrast the horizontal lines and low-pitched roofs of the church itself; and even when — as sometimes happens in the south, for example at Trani — it is connected to the church, the two structures are never seen as part of a unified design. Secondly, Italian Gothic architects never resort to the buttress, the feature which above all in northern churches gives life, vigour and vertical movement to the fabric. Thirdly, the startling use of the cornice in Italian Romanesque and Gothic work instantly recalls classical prototypes, however different the detail, and imparts a strong horizontal character to both the interiors and exteriors of churches. It crowns the tops of walls, as in the Frari church at Venice or in S. Francesco, Brescia, and runs above arcades as in the Cathedrals of Pisa, Orvieto or Enna.

Round arches are preferred to pointed even in the high Gothic period and the arches of arcades, far from performing the functional role they assumed in northern architecture are in Italy frequently held together by iron ties, as are the tracery arches of the second stage of the Doge's Palace, Venice (plate 71). The connecting rods in the arches of the Loggia dei Lanzi, Florence, the interiors of SS. Giovanni e Paolo, Venice, S. Maria Sopra Minerva, Rome, the church of the Frari, Venice, and Milan Cathedral, among numerous other churches and public buildings, make a curious impression of work still in progress and show that the mood in which these builders gothicized was transient. Even in Venice, the city where there were no monuments of classical antiquity to inspire emulation or to hamper the free, spontaneous evolution of the Pointed Style, the enchanting form of Gothic which emerged, characterized principally by the ogee arch, bears the same light-hearted relationship to the earnest Gothic of the north as Strawberry Hill to St Augustine's, Kilburn, London. And the marked tendency in Venice to combine the ogee arch with a basically rectilinear design or to make of it a repeating unit in a long, sweeping horizontal effectively counteracts any vertical tendency implied by the use of the pointed opening.

In the Colosseum the Romans employed tiers of continuous arches in a decorative as well as a constructive manner; the architects of Christian Italy made conspicuous use of arcading as a purely decorative feature. Row upon row of round-headed arcading enlivens the façades of the Duomo, Pisa (plate 59), of S. Michele (plate 57) and the Duomo, Lucca, and of the Cathedral of Pistoia. They entirely cover the circular walls of the Baptistery and Campanile at Pisa (plates 60, 61); arcading in a prominent if less exaggerated form adorns the façades of S. Zeno, Verona, S. Michele, Pavia, S. Pietro and S. Maria Maggiore, Tuscania (plates 48, 49), S. Antonio, Padua, the Duomo, Orvieto and the Cathedrals of Ferrara, Cremona and Trani. These façades are very seldom integral parts of the architectural design of the building as a whole: they are decorative screens displaying marble encrustations and sculptured reliefs and bear little relation to the structure of the nave and aisles behind them. The Gothic compositions which front the Cathedrals of Siena and Orvieto, for instance, were designed quite independently of their relation to the interiors. The façade of S. Michele, Lucca (plate 57) is intended to be looked at only from the front: there is nothing behind the two upper stages and on a night of full moon radiance streams through the wheel window.

Yet if there are structural inconsistencies in these buildings due to conflicting tendencies in the attitude of the designers, the decoration and the materials are all of a magnificence worthy of ancient Rome and entirely in key with the spirit of the Empire. Coloured marbles in black, white, green, pale yellow, peach, rose and gold; glittering mosaics and noble frescoes; sculpture in marble and bronze; mouldings in terracotta and tinted stone; capitals carved with griffins, mermaids, doves and peacocks, serpents, sirens, sphinxes, lions and bulls hidden among luxuriant acanthus leaves; rich marble pilasters; holy water stoups and reliquaries; bronze candelabra; exquisite wrought iron screens; these, each the work of a master in his particular line, are the great delights of Italian churches. It is significant that the only form of decoration which does not attain supreme expression in Italy is that in which the Gothic north excels – stained glass. Thin sheets of marble and alabaster are used, almost to the exclusion of coloured glass, to fill the windows of churches in Italy.

The ornament and furnishing are sometimes so magnificent, so overwhelming, that the architectural forms are blurred. An extreme instance of this is the wonderful interior of St Mark's, Venice, where the effect is of an undulating, expanding sea of gold and subtle, variable, indescribable colour. The strangest elements are united in a single harmony: columns of porphyry, alabaster and *verde antico* from Constantinople and Alexandria; marble panelling from the harem floors of Eastern emperors; lustrous mosaics by Byzantine and Venetian craftsmen; and enamels of all sizes and dates made up into the fabulous screen known as the Pala d'Oro.

Sumptuous decoration, very often incorporating materials and works of art brought from foreign lands, was as typical of ancient Rome as of Early Christian and Gothic Italy and the lavish use of marble for facing exterior walls, yet another feature which distinguishes Italian medieval architecture from that of northern Europe, also derives from Roman practice even though the actual pattern of the marble is always subject to the potent influences of history and geology. The most arresting of these patterns, the stripes of Pisa, Orvieto (plate 67) and Siena, were probably inspired by contact with Eastern art, not only in the wars against the Saracens, but commercially through the annual attendance of Pisan merchants at the Eastern Fair in Jerusalem. The colours of the banded marble were determined by the local stone, cream and rose from Carrara at Pisa, green from Monte Ferrato at Pistoia, Prato and Florence, brilliant black and white from the Apennines at Siena.

Marbles embellish not only the walls but the floors of Italian churches and they are used in the Roman manner, either in the form of small square tesserae to make patterns of figurative decoration, the *opus tesselatum* of antiquity, or in the form of thin sheets of marble cut into shapes to build up the design, as in the *opus sectile* or *opus Alexandrinum* of pre-Christian Italy. These pavements are essentially Italian and here there is often very little distinction between Christian and pagan work. The variety of ingenious patterns in the nave and between the columns of S. Anastasia, Verona, could be exchanged for the diverse arrangements on the floors of the guest chambers at Hadrian's Villa without introducing a single jarring element into either building. In both places the patterns are purely abstract, many of them playing upon cube shapes which seem to start forth three-dimensionally from the floor and which can be read in two entirely different ways like the pictures of the so-called 'optical' painters of today. The delicate circular and wavy mosaic patterns on the floor of S. Pietro, Tuscania, and the multiplicity of geometric designs which make up the pavement of St Mark's, Venice, swelling up and down here with a wild beauty like a petrified sea, have their counterparts in the ravishing patterned borders that frame the figure mosaics at Piazza Armerina and in the designs on the floors of houses at Pompeii and Herculaneum.

The most characteristic decoration of Byzantine churches, the wall mosaic, was also developed from Roman example. Wall mosaics can be seen at Herculaneum, in the House of Neptune and Amphitrite (plate 30), in the Casa dell'Atrio a Mosaico and in the Thermae, in which tesserae of glowing, many-coloured glass are used to form figure subjects, as they were by Christian artists; and here, as in many Byzantine churches, mosaic ornament takes the place of architectural mouldings to frame openings. The discoveries of the past decade at Herculaneum seem to indicate that wall mosaics were more extensively favoured by the Romans than was formerly held to be the case, though perhaps they never clothed entire walls and vaults as they came to do in the later Byzantine churches, such as 'La Martorana', Palermo (plate 54), and St Mark's, Venice (plate 55). The earliest Christian mosaics, however, appear only in the apse and on parts of the walls, as at Ravenna and in the basilicas of Rome. And in style they are at first closely related to classical mosaics, especially, of course, in Rome itself. The beardless, youthful Christ in the apse of S. Vitale, Ravenna, has been likened to Apollo; he also bears a pronounced resemblance to the Orpheus of Piazza Armerina; and the female saints prancing gaily along the upper wall of the nave in S. Apollinare Nuovo, wearing garlands and little red sandals, are first cousins to the dancing girls and vivacious gymnasts of the pagan Sicilian villa. Eastern influence was present in Roman mosaic work before the establishment of Christianity; its effect is felt, as has already been mentioned, in the obscure symbolism of the figure subjects at Piazza Armerina. This influence gradually became more dominant in Byzantine work, where intimacy was replaced by awe and forcefulness in the presentation of the mystery of a transcendental faith. Thus naturalistic perspective was largely abandoned and the smooth-faced Apollonian Christ gave way to a commanding bearded personage possessed of the inscrutable majesty of some ancient Assyrian god. In Italy the most impressive and powerful of these Christianized mosaics are those of the 12th century in Sicily and of the same period at Torcello, near Venice (plate 51). At Torcello the tall, solemn, flame-like figure of the Virgin, isolated on a golden ground, is without parallel in classical art. Those images of dazzling authority, the unrelenting Christ of the *Last*

Judgement at Torcello and the magnetic, terrible countenances that fill the apses of the churches at Cefalu and Monreale with their long, thin noses, hollow cheeks, furrowed brows and piercing black eyes, express an anguish which only faintly and, in the period of its decline, clouds the life-affirming art of the pagan world; it is a bitter, inconsolable grief born of the fatal knowledge of man's predicament and of the torments of sin and conscience.

In the churches built at Palermo and Monreale under Norman rule an extraordinary medley of later influences has been grafted upon a classical heritage. Norman, Byzantine, Islamic and Greco-Roman elements mingle here in an exotic but harmonious whole. If the principal figure at Monreale is entirely Byzantine, the cycles of Old and New Testament scenes on the wall show many incidental resemblances to classical work. Though the artists (probably Greek, so that this building represents a second flowering of the Greek genius in Sicily) sometimes gain their effects by making those figures largest which are farthest away from the spectator, they can be as realistic and skilful in the depiction of movement as the creator of the mosaic of Neptune and Amphitrite at Herculaneum. Nothing could be more spirited than the rendering of Christ driving out the money-changers. The disciples and evangelists wear the togas of pagan philosophers and emperors; and the conception of the female nude with muscular shoulders, rounded thighs and tapering ankles does not differ so widely from that at Piazza Armerina (plate 41) as does Seurat's approach from that of Bonnard. The acanthus, palm and vine motifs of antiquity proliferate everywhere, both in the mosaics, where they consort with Persian prayer-mat designs, and on the capitals of the marble columns. The bronze doors are animated with reliefs by Bonanno Pisano, who was the sculptor of the Porta di San Ranieri at Pisa (plates 64–66). Here, as at Pisa, work which is technically astonishingly close to the bronzes of the Etruscans and Sardinians is altogether Christian in feeling.

The way in which the various forms of the Roman capital and column were adapted in Christian architecture emerges in the plates chosen for this section and in the accompanying notes. The foliage of the Corinthian acanthus and the botanical motifs of late antiquity, whether they hide birds and *amorini* or the symbols of the Passion, predominate. The fascinating subject of the survival of pagan mythology in the Christian era is too complex to receive more than a passing mention here. It forms the theme of a recent illuminating study, *European Art and the Classical Past* by Cornelius Vermeule, Curator of Classical Art at the Boston Museum. But the façade of S. Pietro, Tuscania (plate 48), shows with exceptional clarity how Etruscan imagery was introduced into a Christian building. The snakes, gryphons, dolphins, winged horses and dragons of the Etruscans are all found in the religious art of the Middle Ages in Italy; the pagan chimaera adorns the mosaic floor of the Duomo at Aosta and snarls from the pulpit of S. Ambrogio, Milan. But of all the creatures of classical antiquity the one that flourished most in Christian Italy was the lion (see plates 56–58). The ancestor of the great beasts that so strikingly uphold the pillars of Romanesque porches or lie stretched before them with ravening jaws above a lamb, a calf or a human figure, once guarded the royal palaces of Babylon. Lions travelled across Asia Minor and the Aegean and came to Italy with the Etruscans. By them they were regarded as protectors against the forces of evil; they warded off hostile spirits and demons from the habitations of the dead. Christianity everywhere took over the lion as one of its most important symbolic figures, but the lion portals of Italy are in a class by themselves. The whole conception of these portals, projecting from the façade, is utterly unlike the cavernous, receding compositions favoured elsewhere; and the similarity between the Italian Romanesque lions and those of Etruria, especially in the territory which was once Etruscan, is astounding. The treatment of the manes, the nostrils and jaws and the curious flat heads of the recumbent marble beasts at Ferrara, Modena, Cremona, Nonentola, Verona, San Quirico d'Orcia, Viterbo and Caserta Vecchia is directly derived from Etruscan example. In Christian art the lion is often a symbol of evil held in check by Christ, the Pillar of the Church (plate 56), but it can also stand for Christ and the Resurrection.

The lion portals of Italy are instances of unmistakable pagan influence on style as well as subject matter. They are superbly three-dimensional in an age when sculpture scarcely ever stepped forward from the architectural niche. The climate that encouraged the production of these monumental creatures also fostered the remarkable free-standing sculpture of Antelami in the Baptistery at Parma (plate 70), sculpture which is in no way dependent on architecture and is wholly un-Gothic in feeling. The subjects of his figures, like the lion, do not belong specifically to Christian mythology; these weighty, solid months and seasons, personified and each given a special, appropriate and inevitable character as were the deities of pagan antiquity, come closer to late archaic Greek work than to anything of their own period.

The classical feeling in Antelami's work is probably fortuitous. And the relationship between the bronze reliefs on the doors of S. Zeno, Verona (plates 62, 63), the Duomo, Pisa (plates 64–66), and the Duomo, Troia, on the one hand and Etruscan metalwork on the other may also be instinctive rather than inspired by contact with actual bronzes. The idea of the story relief clearly stemmed from the Roman sculpture on triumphal arches and columns, and the direct inspiration of this classical narrative art is seen in the work of Nicola Pisano, whilst individual figures in his reliefs are based on specific antique prototypes. The reclining Virgin on the Baptistery pulpit at Pisa derives from an Etruscan sepulchral figure; the seated Virgin imitates the Phaedra on a sarcophagus in the Campo Santo at Pisa; and some of the figures on the pulpit in the Duomo of Siena are taken from an Etruscan sarcophagus in the Museo dell'Opera del Duomo. Though less original than the sculpture of Antelami, these reliefs are so deeply felt that they are far more than a pastiche. Like Antelami, Nicola is concerned with the rendering of the human form and with the sense of volume. The achievement of these two great artists foreshadows the future development of sculpture in Italy. It is part of the growing passion for antiquity, the memory and magic of which, as we have seen, never ceased to affect the builders and craftsmen of the peninsula even when they made a show of adopting the Gothic style. Gothic in Italy already partakes of the nature of Renaissance art; the Renaissance differs from it only in that it replaces an intuitive by a conscious revival of classical forms.

Notes on the Plates

The church was built in AD 526–547 by Julianus Argentarius. Honorius, the first ruler of the West after the Roman Empire had been divided on the death of Theodosius I, transferred the capital from Rome to Ravenna in 395. During the reign of Justinian (527–565) Italy and Sicily came once more under the dominion of the Eastern Empire and Ravenna was the seat of the Exarch, the representative of the Byzantine emperors. The mosaics were probably set up at about the time of this event, in 539.

Byzantine work in Italy is on the whole far closer to classical example than that of the Eastern Empire. The mosaic shown here, the subjects of which are *The Hospitality of Abraham* and *Abraham Sacrificing Isaac*, is neither rigidly frontal nor severely stylized. With its fresh colouring and naturalistic rendering of the tree and the delightful plants, it differs less from such pagan Roman mosaics as those of Piazza Armerina (plate 41) than from its companion pieces at S. Vitale: the famous compositions of Justinian and Theodora with their retainers, in which Eastern influence predominates. Both at Pompeii and Herculaneum there are many examples of bird and still-life groups resembling those in the spandrels of these Ravenna arches. The replacement of architectural mouldings round the lunette and arches by bands of mosaic was common in Roman wall mosaics and there is an example of it in the Herculaneum interior shown in plate 30.

The capitals of the columns are superficially quite unlike antique models though they were evolved from the Roman composite capital. The carved decoration, instead of standing out in bold relief, as in Roman work, is all contained within the outline of the capital, sharply incised and emphatically patterned rather than sculptured. The deep abacus above the actual capital, forming a second capital or impost, derives from the classic entablature which is replaced here by an arcade. The winged lambs which strongly recall the winged horses on the columns of the Temple of Mars Ultor, Rome, contrast with the incised ornament of the capitals. These amply modelled reliefs were carved locally while the capitals themselves were imported from the Sea of Marmora region.

The Benedictine Monastery of Monreale was built between 1174 and 1182 by William II. Sicily had been in the hands of the Byzantine emperors from the time of Justinian until the 9th century when the island came under Arab rule; then in the 11th century it was conquered by Robert Guiscard of Hauteville and his youngest brother Roger. Under the three great Norman kings Roger II, William I and William II the diverse elements in Sicilian art were all united in a remarkable harmony which is perfectly reflected in the great churches of the period, where classical, Muslim, Byzantine and Norman features are fused into a unique and fascinating whole. The character of this compound art is vividly illustrated by the coupled columns of the colonnade at Monreale. The design of the pillars in plate 45, entwined with vines, is directly descended from the flowing decoration of leaves and fruit which so often embellishes Roman shafts and pilasters, naturalistically as on the fountain column at Herculaneum (plate 30) or in a more formal manner as on the arch at Benevento (plate 19 and 21). The capitals show characteristic Romanesque sculpture combined with the classical palmette ornament. On the right, diagonal bands of glittering mosaic and deeply cut Romanesque zigzags support Corinthianesque capitals and Moorish stilted arches.

45, 47
COLUMNS IN THE
CLOISTERS AT
MONREALE
(*Palermo, Sicily*)

S. Apollinare in Classe was built on the site of a temple of Apollo by Julianus Argentarius and consecrated in 549. The columns are of rich marble surmounted by capitals the fantastic design of which is governed by pagan precedent, while transforming it. It is based on the Roman composite capital though the classical acanthus decoration has undergone a strange transformation; the leaves beneath Ionic volutes and egg-and-dart motifs are irregularly disposed, more tightly furled and curiously compressed.

46
RAVENNA
S. APOLLINARE
IN CLASSE:
ARCADE

The church was begun in the 8th century and altered and completed in the 11th and 12th centuries. It was built over the remains of a Roman temple which had itself taken the place of an Etruscan sanctuary.

The exquisite pattern of this façade synthesizes the most incongruous elements into a homogeneous whole. The entire façade teems with life: grotesque monsters, reptiles,

48
TUSCANIA
S. PIETRO:
FAÇADE

beasts, birds, saints, and angels run riot within a framework of pilaster, frieze and pediment that might well be those of an antique temple. The attached columns, completely covered with a motif like the Egyptian lotus-bud, impart an oriental flavour to the façade which is enhanced by much of the detail of the carving and by the huge three-dimensional bulls at the feet of the pilasters which immediately recall the bulls of the Etruscans, who have left their imprint all over this part of Italy. The ornament is of white marble, richly embellished with mosaic, and gleams like bejewelled ivory against the dark red-brown masonry of the wall itself. The acanthus leaf is a prominent component of the decoration: it forms the basis of the moulding round the large wheel window (a characteristic feature of the Romanesque façade), the central spokes of which are miniature Norman columns; it burgeons on the spiralling vines round the right-hand opening and proliferates under the opening on the left. Here the classical motif is combined with images of saints, angels and the Lamb of God in mosaic-encrusted roundels, in the manner of Byzantine ivories. But between each of these Christian symbols, which themselves are half caricatured, are smaller roundels filled with grotesque heads which are closely allied to Etruscan representations of gorgons and demons; and below the left-hand opening is a slab which is actually Etruscan, carved with a relief of a Tyrrhenian dancer. It may well have come from the original sanctuary on this spot. To balance this relief there is a terrifying figure on the right who bears so close a resemblance to the Etruscan Geryon, the three-faced demon of the underworld, that his presence in this Etruscan site must be due to a continuing tradition. Like the devils of the Etruscan inferno he is crowned by flames and clasps a serpent to his bosom, symbol of the powers of hell. Out of his sensual mouths grow rank ramblers, among the giant leaves and flowers of which sport little demons with human heads and bird bodies and pointed head-dresses like Mithraic caps. On either side of the three-headed monster droop the seed-heads of poppies, another pagan symbol of the kingdom of the dead. The creeper rises in coils to a second triple-headed demon above the window, whose brows are wreathed in leaves.

The use of the trifacial demon of Etruscan origin as a grim caricature of the Trinity became widespread in the later Middle Ages. The authorities of the Church repeatedly protested against this symbol of demonic character, but it was only finally prohibited by Pope Urban VIII at the beginning of the 17th century.

49, 50
TUSCANIA S. MARIA
MAGGIORE:
CENTRE DOORWAY
AND INTERIOR

This church stands close to that shown on the preceding page, outside the town of Tuscania, beside the ruins of the former episcopal palace and flanked by two high battered towers. The churches are deserted today; the Piazza in front of S. Pietro and the narrow road between the two buildings are thickly overgrown with grass. S. Maria Maggiore, like S. Pietro, was founded in the 8th century, but was more extensively altered than its companion during the 12th century. Like the façade of S. Pietro, that of S. Maria Maggiore is built of the local stone while all the ornamental features, the pilasters and carving of the doorway and the arcading, are of marble. Both façades show the concentration on ornamental detail which characterizes Italian Romanesque and Gothic art, while architecturally both are governed by classical tradition. This tradition is also predominant in the external detail of S. Maria Maggiore in the capitals and the mouldings. The figure sculpture, the Virgin and Child (placed off-centre), the groups depicting the entry into Jerusalem and the Massacre of the Innocents, and the figures of the Lamb of God and of St Peter and St Paul below, are reminiscent of those of S. Trophîme at Arles – both in their bold almost three-dimensional quality and in their reliance on classical precedent.

The interior, architecturally a basilica with a broad nave and timber roof, is unexpectedly light; it is also full of colour. The piers show the remains of frescoes whilst the east end of the nave, the apse and the ciborium are covered with paintings. Though the atmosphere of this abandoned church is one of rare serenity, it is again full of contrasting influences. The Corinthianesque columns support round-arched arcades instead of an entablature and the decoration that patterns the whole of the marble font exhibits motifs of classical, Moorish and Romanesque derivation; the frescoes of the Apostles in the apse and of the Evangelists seated at their desks on the ceiling of the ciborium are Byzantine in character. The ciborium itself has scalloped, Saracenic arches resting on antique columns. The huge fresco of the Last Judgement above the apse has many affinities with Etruscan paintings of the underworld. The Prince of Hell is presented, as in the relief on the façade of S. Pietro (plate 48), with snakes winding about him, swallowing the bodies of the damned.

This mosaic of the Last Judgement dates from the late 12th century and belongs to the post-iconoclast age when some of the finest decorations on a large scale were produced in those parts of Italy which came under Byzantine influence, namely Venice and Sicily. This powerful work, executed by Greek artists and far grander and more sublime in conception than the lunette at Ravenna (plate 44), is characterized by an essentially mystical approach. Whereas the work at Ravenna has much in common with antique mosaics, this dramatic composition is governed by an entirely different attitude. The laws of perspective have been flung aside and the principal figure is a giant dominating the whole scene, a compelling, forbidding, implacable Divinity. The airiness of the Ravenna mosaic, born of the tree and the springing plants, has been replaced by the grandeur and supra-terrestrial lustre of dull gold. Whereas at Ravenna the delighted affirmation of life expressed in the realism of the images is threatened by no more than the merest shadow of doubt, the stern Pantocrator of Torcello and the

51
TORCELLO
DUOMO:
MOSAIC ON
ENTRANCE WALL

awesome angel whose black orbs transfix and follow each person who enters the church insist that all manifestations of the physical world are illusory and that reality lies beyond them.

52, 53
BARI
S. NICOLA:
FAÇADE AND
INTERIOR

Bari was a town of importance during the rule of the Norman kings in southern Italy and Sicily and the cathedral, begun under Count Roger and completed in the 12th century under William II, has more in common with the Romanesque churches of the north than with those of this period in southern Italy. It is constructed on the lines of a Roman basilica and it has the typical Italian projecting porch with columns upheld by lions. The austere façade, however, is a strongly vertical design, without the cornices or friezes which usually divide Italian church fronts into storeys and invest the composition with a marked horizontality. S. Nicola is also conceived as an architectural whole, which is not the case with most Italian Romanesque and Gothic churches. The façade is not merely a screen but part of an integrated composition: the church is surrounded on all four sides by planned open spaces paved with granite sets and banded with the white stone of the district in radiating patterns; and the building is meant to be looked at from every side. Classical influence is nevertheless present, especially in the columns of both the interior and exterior of the church.

The severity of the interior, relieved only by the sprouting Corinthianesque foliage of the capitals, is in startling contrast to the sumptuous gilded Baroque ceiling added in the 17th century. The broad nave is spanned by three arches supported on pillars of dove-coloured marble with glistering white capitals. A Romanesque tabernacle stands over the altar; it has a two-tiered octagonal cover, carried at each stage by diminutive Romanesque columns which, like the four main pillars, are of pink marble with delicately carved capitals where angels peer through curling acanthus leaves. Behind this tabernacle, at the end of the apse, is an 11th-century bishop's throne of marble. This feature was of pagan origin and was taken over in Early Christian churches with the basilican plan. In Roman basilicas it was the seat of the Judex.

54
PALERMO, SICILY
'LA MARTORANA'

This 12th-century church is a characteristic Sicilian blend of Saracenic, Byzantine and Romanesque art, though here the Byzantine element is strongest. The building is in the form of a Greek cross with a central dome and is completely lined with mosaics except for the choir which, redecorated in flamboyant baroque, intrudes harshly on the mysterious and inspiring atmosphere of this glittering interior. The mosaics, the work of Greek craftsmen, are brilliant in colour, the figures shining on a ground of dusky gold. The colour is so magnificent and the bands of abstract design between the figure subjects are so prominent, that the spectator is scarcely aware of the architectural form. The huge Pantocrator in the dome hovers overhead, remote and majestic; the Apostles proclaim Gospel truths, and galaxies of angels with stiff blue and white wings, long slender bodies, extremely short legs, great almond eyes and snaky locks incline their heads to look down on some New Testament scene; or bend awkwardly forward to assist at an episode in the life of the Virgin. Though their fabulous blue-edged, cubist pinions look far too solid and weighty for flight, the church seems to be full of the rush of wings and these shimmering beings, whose calm, grave faces show no trace of either anger or compassion, truly seem to be creatures of another world, worthy instruments of the great being in the dome.

Two of the mosaic scenes in this interior are of historical interest. In one of them Christ crowns the Emperor Roger, with his misshapen nose, and in the other the donor, Admiral George of Antioch, kneels at the feet of the Virgin (the church is also known as S. Maria dell'Ammiraglio). The magnificent columns of golden-yellow marble are the most classical feature of 'La Martorana'; the acanthus-leaved capitals are indistinguishable from late Roman work.

Rebuilt when Venice was under the influence of Byzantium, St Mark's, originally a basilica, was designed to resemble the Church of the Apostles, Constantinople: the plan is that of a Greek cross surmounted by five domes. The mosaics in the interior are of roughly the same date as those of 'La Martorana' and here again all architectural detail is subordinated to the decorative effect of the expanses of gold and brilliant colour extending in a continuous surface over vault and dome. Mosaics depicting Old and New Testament subjects adorn the whole of the church above the level of the crown of the main arches, while the lower parts of the walls are encrusted with slabs of marble of all sizes, arranged without apparent design like one huge abstract collage. The domed cover of the great double lectern echoes and emphasizes the shapes of the cupolas.

**55
VENICE
S. MARCO**

Lions play a strange part in Romanesque art and nowhere are they more in evidence than in Italy, where magnificent growling beasts support the columns of porches or crouch in front of the church, sometimes holding lambs or human beings in their forepaws or in their fearsome jaws. They often symbolize the forces of evil, though they sometimes also represent David as the Lion of Judah. The column from the portal of the Duomo at Ferrara (56), standing for Christ, the Pillar of the Church, is supported by the bowed figure of an infidel who rests on the back of a lion, the symbol here of evil overcome. The sculptor is one of the earliest in Italy to be known by name. He was Master Niccolo and the work dates from 1135.

**56-58
ROMANESQUE
LIONS**

The flat-headed lion of Asiatic appearance from the portal arch of the Duomo, Caserta Vecchia (58), has clear affinities with the lion on the Etruscan tomb shown in plate 17. He is crouching over a man and personifies the Devil with a victim. The carving dates from the early 12th century.

In the inlaid marble decoration on the façade of S. Michele, Lucca (57), lions are also in evidence. The gable of this façade is merely a screen to support the elaborate ornament. The use of arcading to cover the whole of the upper part of the composition, thus transforming a feature of constructive architectural origin into a decorative motif, is typical of the Romanesque churches of central Italy. Byzantine influence was strong at Pisa, where the style of S. Michele originated, and is seen here in the mosaic-encrusted columns and the green-and-white inlaid marble friezes where the oriental designs of the famous Lucca velvets are translated into stone. Both the textiles and the façade are of the same period, the first half of the 13th century. The church was begun in 1143 but the façade was a later addition.

59-61
PISA
DUOMO,
BAPTISTERY DOME
AND CAMPANILE

These three buildings together with the Campo Santo form one of the most famous groups in the world. It is still an unforgettable experience to come upon these dazzling, diverse and yet wonderfully harmonious shapes rising from the wide stretch of close-cut grass and clover in which they stand apart from the rest of the town.

The Duomo (59) was built in the second half of the 11th century, the Campanile (61) dates from 1174 with a belfry added only in 1315 because of subsidence; and the Baptistery (60) was begun by Diotisalvi in 1152, continued by Nicola and Giovanni Pisano in the following century and completed in the 14th century.

The decorative use of arcading, already remarked in S. Michele, Lucca (plate 57), is a conspicuous feature of all three buildings. The Duomo is a basilica and the façade recalls that of a Roman structure. Although the treatment is different, the basic outline is extraordinarily like that of a transverse section of the Basilica of Constantine. The image of a classical temple is also suggested by the high lateral gables, and the capitals and mouldings recall Roman work although the motifs are applied here with a vivacity of line and curve which is as subtly distinct from classical practice as is the decorative striping of the walls with bands of red and white marble. The repetition of the arcade motif on the façades of the Duomo and the Campanile imparts to these structures a pure, regular rhythm and a horizontal emphasis which are essentially classical. The Baptistery was originally animated by an identical rhythm but the flickering Gothic elements added in the 14th century introduce a wayward accent, though the great breadth of the building counteracts the aspiring movement. The massive busts in the fretted niches, the work of the school of the classically-inspired Nicola and Giovanni

Pisano, whether or not executed by the masters themselves, add dignity and substance to the structure.

The reliefs from the door of S. Zeno, Verona (62, 63) depict two legends of the saint. Those from the Porta S. Ranieri at the Duomo, Pisa, show the Flight into Egypt (64) and the Massacre of the Innocents (65); plate 66 is a detail of another relief from this door. The doors of both churches consist of a series of individual scenes, each separately cast. The narrative relief as an art form derived from the sculptured chronicles of the Romans on their triumphal arches and on such works as the columns of Trajan and Marcus Aurelius. But the expressive style of these bronze reliefs is immediately reminiscent not of Roman but of Etruscan and Sardinian work. The large heads at the corners of the panels at Verona are astonishingly close to the masks on Etruscan Canopic vases. The fascinating resemblances between works so far apart in time may not be entirely fortuitous: both Pisa and Verona were once Etruscan cities, and the relations of Pisa with Sardinia were close at the time when these bronzes were made. The reliefs on the door of the Porta S. Ranieri date from the late 12th century and are the work of Bonanno Pisano. The S. Zeno door is a little earlier.

62–66
BRONZE RELIEFS
TWELFTH CENTURY

The Duomo at Orvieto, whose north wall is shown in plate 67, was built in 1290–1316. That at Florence (plate 68 shows the exterior of the octagon with its apses and chapels) was begun in 1296. Both buildings were designed by Arnolfo di Cambio. The distinguishing feature of the architecture, as emphasized in these photographs, is the marble decoration in zebra stripes and in panels of inlay work. The use of marble for facing walls distinguishes both the Romanesque and Gothic architecture of central Italy from that of the rest of Europe and the predilection for stripes in Tuscany originated in Pisa. As a great naval power, Pisa took the lead during the 11th century in the wars against the infidels; the Pisans defeated the Saracens three times at Tunis and in 1062 they captured Palermo. It was perhaps this contact with the Saracens which accounted for the characteristic Pisan addiction to striped marbles.

In both these great cathedrals of the Gothic period Roman traditions persist. The emphatic horizontals of the marble ornament neutralize any tendency towards Gothic verticality; there are no buttresses and the windows are round-arched even when they are surmounted by pointed canopies; and Orvieto, despite its Gothic façade, is firmly based on the basilican plan.

67, 68
MARBLE
DECORATION
AT ORVIETO AND
FLORENCE

69
PARMA
BAPTISTERY

The octagonal 12th-century Baptistery with its two-storeyed ring of rose-coloured marble columns was modelled on that of Constantine in Rome, which was built in the 5th century not by Constantine but by Sixtus III. There the columns are antique, purloined from the ruins of ancient Rome. Here at Parma the columns owe much to classical example, though the symbolism of the figurative carving is Christian or Christianized. The capital in the foreground of the photograph is carved with the favourite Italian Romanesque motif of lions as demons with their victims.

70
STATUE OF
JANUARY, BY
BENEDETTO
ANTELAMI
(*Baptistery, Parma*)

The most remarkable feature of the Baptistery at Parma is the series of free-standing sculptures by Benedetto Antelami of the months and seasons arranged all round the octagonal room. The artist was working on them from 1196 onwards, probably after a period spent in Provence at Saint-Gilles and at Arles. The sculpture at S. Trophîme and Saint-Gilles is inspired by late antique example: in Antelami's work the influence goes deeper. These figures are weightier than the French carvings; they are also informed with a profound feeling for the human body that is far more Renaissance than Gothic in character. The statues are of marble; the one shown here represents January and, Janus-like, has two heads facing in opposite directions to symbolize the winter solstice.

The fresco of the Madonna della Carita dating from the 15th century – more than two hundred years later, therefore, than the sculptured figure in front of it – emphasizes by its feeble grasp of form and weak drawing the astonishing plastic achievement of Antelami.

71
VENICE
DOGE'S PALACE
AND THE PIAZZETTA

The enchanting style of this building, which set the mode for the palaces of the aristocratic Venetian families, has no counterpart elsewhere in Italy. The whole scheme of columned and pointed arcading combined with a long, sweeping, horizontal movement makes up that unique and magical combination of Gothic detail and classical line known as Venetian Gothic. The sturdy aspect of the second tier of arcades is an essential part of the design, for only thus could the huge upper storey of unbroken wall space (only fractionally visible in the photograph) appear to rest on a sufficiently solid support. This façade was built between 1424 and 1442 to the design of Pietro Bascio and Filippo Calendario. Although the pointed arch is the most conspicuous feature of the composition, the Doge's Palace is not Gothic in the northern sense. There is no approach to the constructional system of pier, arch and buttress; the mouldings are of extreme simplicity; the cusps of the tracery are square-ended and each is fancifully adorned with a gay little ball of red marble. Moreover, the carving of the capitals is uniform throughout and thus the design presents a seemingly infinite succession of the same features in shaft and tracery. This effect — alien to true Gothic, the essence of which is diversity — demonstrates the compelling power and beauty of perfect regularity as convincingly as any work of classical antiquity. The regularity creates a delightful harmony between the roundels, the curving ogees and pointed arches, and the rectilinear shapes of the geometrical paving of Istrian limestone stretched like a carpet beside the Palace.

The column surmounted by a 6th-century Byzantine lion, shown here outlined against the sky and water, is one of two monoliths which came to Venice as pillage from Constantinople and now stand at the edge of the Piazzetta.

This flight of steps leads up to the Piazza del Duomo from the Baptistery, which was the work of Giacomo di Mino del Pellicciaio and was built in 1382. The elaborate portal at the head of the steps is a characteristic example of the Italian version of Gothic: the pointed elements are more ornamental than structural and the actual opening is round-headed; the vertical effect of the canopy work is minimized by the forceful horizontal lines of the black and white marble striping and bands of ornament. The architect of this portal, as of the lower, late 13th-century part of the Duomo façade, was Giovanni Pisano.

72
SIENA
PIAZZA DEL
DUOMO:
STEPS AND PORTAL

The Palazzo stands on the crest of an escarpment in a vast undulating landscape not far from the source of the Arno, with a distant view of Bibbiena. Built in the last quarter of the 13th century, this stronghold resembles the Palazzo del Podesta (or Bargello) in Florence with its lofty angle tower and fortified façade. A drawbridge leads to a gatehouse and a grassy, crenellated enclosure in which the battlemented Palazzo rises, grave and severe with little external ornament except for a sculptured lion over the portal carved by a local artist, Jacopo di Baldassare Turriane. The cortile, designed by Arnolfo di Cambio in 1291, is conspicuous for its magnificent stone stairway, the balusters of which are restrained Corinthianesque columns. The Palazzo was for centuries the home of the Counts Guido, among whom Simone da Battifolle achieved fame by defending the freedom of Florence in 1343. From 1440 when Count Francesco, the last Guido, was banished for aiding the Duke of Milan in the war against Venice, the Palazzo belonged to the Republic of Florence and was inhabited by administrators from Florence.

73
POPPI
PALAZZO
PRETORIA:
CORTILE

74
ENNA
DUOMO

This church was built in the 14th century and restored two hundred years later. The pointed arches and the extraordinary bases of the columns are almost the only signs of Gothic in this noble interior. And these sculptured bases instantly recall the religion of nature-worship with which the site of the Duomo was connected in antiquity. A temple of Demeter stood here and all the creatures closest to the earth – reptiles, lizards, toads, frogs, nameless monsters with human heads and the bodies of snakes, serpents and scaly dragons – writhe under the weight of the massive pillars, symbolizing the kingdom of Aidoneus as well as demons subdued by the power of the Church. The ebony hue of these columns, fashioned of black alabaster, contrasts with the brilliant white of the walls and the coloured marbles of the paving. The capitals burgeoning with acanthus leaves and garlands from which peer winged horses, twin-tailed mermen, doves, dolphins and masks, the foliage designs on the arcade walls and the rich, strikingly horizontal cornice are all alien to the spirit of Gothic.

Plates 44-74

47

54

59

60

61

62

63

71

The Renaissance

THE PLATES IN THE PREVIOUS SECTION mirrored the continuous, if half-unconscious struggle of Italian architects and craftsmen throughout the Middle Ages to return to a classical expression of art. Antelami, as we have seen, instinctively produced free-standing sculpture of a markedly classical temper, churches such as the Duomo at Pisa displayed the clarity and horizontality of the works of antiquity, and motifs which originated in pagan decoration and symbolized pagan beliefs were used to ornament Christian sanctuaries. Nicola Pisano's deliberate copying of the details of classical sculpture has been mentioned. And there was another remarkable instance of an attempt in the Gothic period to re-create classical forms in the triumphal arch Frederick II of Hohenstaufen built at Capua. It was surmounted by a figure of the Emperor and decorated with reliefs of his victories in the Roman manner, and with the head of Jupiter and a personification of the city of Capua. The head of the god, all that survives of this astonishing work, is entirely in the antique tradition; and there was no trace of Christian feeling in any detail of this arch.

But more than an innate sympathy for the architecture of the classical past, more than nostalgia for the greatness of Imperial Rome, was required to bring about the revolution in art and thought known as the Renaissance. The movement was preceded by the study of ancient literature and it is to Petrarch that the first impulse towards the revival of learning is due. The spark he kindled burst into a flame: regard for classical learning grew into a passion that strikes us as extraordinary. It was symptomatic of Renaissance enthusiasm for Greek and Latin writers that the humanist Marsilio Ficino should burn a lamp before the bust of Plato as of a saint, and that the discovery in 1413 in his native Padua of some bones supposed, no doubt erroneously, to be those of the Roman historian, Livy, should create an outburst of fervour that can only be described as religious. The sacred remains were enshrined in the Palazzo della Ragione where they still repose.

This enthusiasm for the ancient world soon absorbed all interests and was accompanied by a revolt against ecclesiastical tyranny. For the first time since it was officially established the Christian religion ceased to be the exclusive inspiration of artists and architects. Of the photographs of Early Christian, Romanesque and Gothic work reproduced in this book, all but two exhibit ecclesiastical architecture and decoration. The plates that accompany this section emphasize the preoccupation of Renaissance builders and designers not only with churches but with sumptuous palaces and pleasure gardens. Appreciation of the beauties of landscape and nature, first voiced by Aeneas Silvius, later Pope Pius II, was but one aspect of a new philosophy which stressed the importance of the individual and the delights of physical existence as opposed to the medieval concern with abstract theological argument and the asceticism of medieval Christianity. The classical figurative motifs which had crept into Romanesque and Gothic art in the guise of devils now took their place in painting and sculpture beside the Madonna and the Saints, not as objects of devotion, but as vital symbols of the living inspiration of antiquity. And the revival of Roman architecture was pursued with as much ardour as the cultivation of ancient literature.

To this end the ruins of Imperial Rome became the object of careful study and for the first time collections were made of classical antiquities. Mantegna, Ghiberti and Donatello all owned famous collections. Mantegna's assemblage of marbles was so highly regarded that in 1483 Lorenzo de' Medici thought it worth a special visit. Cosimo de' Medici had made an extensive collection which Lorenzo enlarged and displayed in his garden near the monastery of S. Marco. It was a grove of *accademìa*, full of statues, busts and specimens of ancient art placed under the superintendence of Bertoldo, assistant to Donatello, who by that time was too old for work. The humanist Niccolo Niccoli owned a small gallery containing marbles, vases, coins and engraved gems; and Bracciolini Poggio even employed an agent, Francesco di Pistoia, to procure works from Greece to add to his museum. 'My chamber,' he wrote in a letter to Francesco, 'is surrounded by busts in marble, one of which is whole and elegant. The others are indeed mutilated, and some of them are indeed noseless, yet they are such as may please a good artist . . . believe me, my friend, you cannot confer a greater favour on me than by returning laded with such works.'

Another element in the Renaissance cult of the antique was the writing of treatises on the various arts. Alberti was the first of a long line of architects who wrote about building: Bramante, Serlio, Vignola, Palladio and Scamozzi, to name but a few. Alberti not only laid down the rules about architecture, but like Leonardo also compiled a treatise on painting; and Piero della Francesca was the author of a famous essay on perspective. In 1414, in the monastery of St Gall, Poggio discovered a manuscript which at once riveted the attention of all enthusiasts for the classical past. It was a pedantic work by the Roman architect and author Vitruvius Pollio, who was in charge of the Engines of War under Marcus Aurelius; whilst it threw considerable light on the practice of antiquity, its effect, not only on Italian Renaissance architecture but on subsequent developments everywhere in Europe, bore no relation to its merits. Vitruvius's *De Architectura* changed the attitude of architects to their work as radically as Galileo's startling discovery that the earth was not the centre of the universe changed the intellectual perspective of the times. Vitruvius explained that the buildings of ancient Rome were designed in certain proportions to a module, which was the radius of the column at its base. It seemed as though the whole secret of classical architecture had been laid bare and that it was only necessary to follow the precepts of Vitruvius for the art of ancient Rome to live again. But the manuscript Poggio had unearthed was not published until 1486. Even when, in the early 15th century, fresh, untrammelled pleasure in ancient example was tempered by a desire to apply correct rules, inspired interpretation never yielded to slavish imitation.

The emancipated attitude of Renaissance artists towards the work of the classical past is illustrated by Michelangelo's use of one of the pillars of the Roman temple of Castor and Pollux to make a pedestal for the equestrian statue of Marcus Aurelius in the Piazza del Campidoglio. Another obvious instance of the freedom with which Vitruvian rules were applied is that although the classic Roman orders of architecture, the Tuscan, Doric, Ionic, Corinthian and Composite, which had survived with strange mutations throughout the Middle Ages, were correctly rendered by Renaissance architects, they treated capitals with infinite variety and fantasy. Renaissance angle volutes may end in tight scrolls, as at S. Maria dei Miracoli, Venice, which suddenly burst into leaf and flower – not of any plant seen on the capitals of the ancients, but of the formalized but minutely observed hyssop. The volutes may also be replaced by human figures and mythological beings as at S. Spirito, Florence, or by cornucopias on either side of vase shapes from which spring leaves and fruits as in the cortile of the Palazzo Gondi.

The effect of the new current of thought and feeling was manifested, as this brief reference to Renaissance capitals suggests, not by attempts to copy the work of antiquity, but in the release of a burst of creative energy, bewildering in its luxuriance, and in an audacity of imagination that had previously been held in check by a style that was never congenial to the Italian temper. And although architects, sculptors and painters embraced classical forms and classical motifs with the utmost earnestness and sense of purpose, there was no sudden break with the past. The grand and astonishing façade Alberti added to S. Andrea, Mantua, with its immense central entrance arching right up to the pediment which itself is surmounted by an extraordinary arched and coffered open gable – as monumental a design as anything produced by the Romans – is perhaps unique among early Renaissance buildings in that it cannot be remotely compared to any Gothic work in Italy. The frontispiece with which the same architect embellished S. Maria Novella, Florence (plate 75), certainly introduces a new feature in the scroll ornaments linking nave and aisles. But in its use of inlaid marbles in the form of stripes and panels – which follows Romanesque and Gothic practice (see pages 99, 111) – and in the general design, it is not remarkably different from the façade of S. Miniato al Monte which goes back to the 11th and 12th centuries. The familiar two-light window of the Gothic period, divided by slender pilasters, survives in Alberti's Rucellai Palace as well as in the great palazzo Maiano built for the Strozzis (plate 77); although both these austere buildings exhibit a breadth and grandeur of style unknown in medieval secular architecture. The Ducal Palace at Urbino (plate 78) also achieves a balanced, though quite different harmony between medieval and classical elements in a combination of Gothic irregularity of plan with massive classical simplicity of treatment. Brunelleschi's giant dome poised on its octagonal drum above the Duomo of Florence determines the whole visual character of the city and dominates the entire panorama seen from S. Miniato or Fiesole, vying in size with the surrounding hills. It is like a symbol both of Florence, which more than any other place has become identified with the birth of the Renaissance, and of the movement itself. Yet it is based on the rib system of construction which is essentially Gothic, although the ribs are hidden in a double shell and there are no supporting arches. The same architect's lovely church of S. Lorenzo, also in Florence, follows classical example more closely, and in the unusual form of its columns, surmounted by supporting entablature blocks like those of the Baths of Caracalla and the Baths of Diocletian, it shows the fruits of Brunelleschi's visit to Rome in 1403, made with the express purpose of studying Roman architecture at the fountain-head.

In Venice the architecture of the Middle Ages changed by even more imperceptible degrees into that of the Renaissance, and the family likeness between such earlier buildings as the Palazzo Pisani or the Ca' d'Oro and the Palazzo Corner Spinelli or the Palazzo Vendramini needs no underlining. The composition of the medieval façades is already firmly horizontal; in the later palaces the general lines of the design remain unaltered, while in the shape of the windows Gothic merely gives way to quasi-Gothic. The structure and ornament of the marble-encrusted S. Maria dei Miracoli (plates 81, 82) make use of Byzantine features. And (to anticipate later developments for a moment) the most sumptuous of the mature Renaissance buildings in Venice, the Library of St Mark by Sansovino with its double row of long-lined arcades, is designed to harmonize with the Ducal Palace on the opposite side of the Piazzetta (plate 71). The architect's familiarity with Vitruvius has not curbed his imagination, which is expressed in a feature of enchanting fantasy and individuality, the rich and enormously wide frieze in which oval windows pattern a dazzling array of cherubs and festoons of fruit and flowers with spots of deepest shade.

We have seen with what zest and imagination the decorative arts were pursued during the Romanesque and Gothic periods. Renaissance artists indulged in this tendency with equal enthusiasm, sometimes with the excessive exuberance which is a recurring element in Italian art, and which was not always quelled by their devotion to antique example. The façade of the Certosa of Pavia, for example, though full of delightful detail (plate 84) is not only as little integrated into the design of the church behind it as any Gothic frontispiece, but is covered with a confusion of ornament which even the strong parallel lines of two arcaded galleries running right across the composition fail to control. The design is closed on either side by projecting turrets adorned with tiers of terracotta sculpture in niches and crowned by spires; a hooded doorway supported on coupled classical columns marks the centre of the façade and above it one of the arcades is surmounted by a pedimented feature enclosing a rose window. The uppermost stage, which is unexpectedly square and merely a screen with nothing behind it, consists of the second series of arcades and a lavish cornice. Every inch of the remaining surface space is decorated – with window cases, the mullions of which, minutely carved, swell outwards like branching candelabra; with arabesques, festoons, scroll work, reliefs, statues and inlaid marbles.

The mosaic pavings of the 12th and 13th centuries, which were largely based on the work of the Romans, had their counterparts in Renaissance churches and palaces. The chief distinction between the pavements of the two periods was that Renaissance floor mosaicists introduced figure subjects as the Romans had done; figure subjects which had been abandoned by medieval artists in favour of purely abstract designs. The figurative floor decorations in the Cathedral of Siena are among the most striking of Renaissance pavings, the work here being of the kind the Romans called 'opus sectile', a variety of marble marquetry executed with amazing skill. They include seven octagonal panels enclosed in borders exactly resembling those encircling the roundels on the façade of S. Maria dei Miracoli (plate 81), and showing figures representing the Seven Ages: Infantia, Pueritia, Adolescentia, Juventus with a hawk, Virilitas with a book, Senectus walking in a trim garden and Decrepitus on his crutches approaching the tomb. But more remarkable than these panels, the over-all effect of which is still geometrical, is a group of more than fifty large marble inlay compositions of Biblical and mythological subjects with almost life-size figures. A number of artists worked on them, among them Matteo di Giovanni and Beccafumi, who is the most original of them all.

The use of terracotta, inherited from the Etruscans, was mentioned earlier in these pages; it was continued and developed by Renaissance artists, whose architectural decorations in this medium were the source of some of the most repellent effects of 19th-century builders in northern Europe. Bramante used terracotta for the chaste ornament of the apse of S. Maria delle Grazie, Milan. The façade of the Oratory of S. Bernardino at Perugia, designed and executed by Agostino di Duccio between 1457 and 1461, is a masterpiece of relief work in this material; and the mouldings on the Ospedale Maggiore, Milan, by Antonio Filarete with three-dimensional figures leaning from roundels and rich friezes of scrolly foliage which turns into hounds, serpents, dragons and leafy-haired *amorini* directly recall Etruscan imagery. Filarete provides an interesting instance of the Renaissance artist's disregard of fixed rules, for he was not only the creator of this spontaneous decoration and the architect of the graceful building itself, but the writer of an absurdly pedantic treatise on the design of an ideal city.

The extension by Renaissance artists of terracotta as a medium for portraiture and free-standing sculpture establishes another link between them and the Etruscans. The best of the Florentine painted and enamelled terracottas, the work of Benedetto da Maiano, of Luca della Robbia, Verrocchio, Antonio Rossellino and Matteo Civitale, are the descendants of the Etruscan tomb figures and of groups such as the Ariadne in Naxos of the 3rd century BC in the Museo Civico, Bologna.

Other forms of Renaissance sculpture show parallels and affinities with the work of antiquity, but again, as with architecture, there is no sharp line of demarcation between the work of the Middle Ages and that of men like Ghiberti and Donatello. Ghiberti's reliefs on the doors of the Florence Baptistery with their landscape and architectural settings and Donatello's dramatic relief of the Feast of Herod in the Baptistery at Siena carry the narrative art of Nicola Pisano even closer to such Roman reliefs as those on the Arch of Titus in Rome. And if the reliefs on the doors of S. Zeno, Verona, and of the Baptistery, Pisa (plates 62–66), recall Etruscan bronzes, the resemblance between Donatello's free-standing sculpture and Etruscan work is still more arresting. It is impressively illustrated by a comparison between the head of the Etruscan bronze of a reclining man in the Museo Archeologico, Florence, and the heads of Donatello's early David in marble and still more of his St George (both in the Bargello, Florence). Figures such as that of the Orator and heads such as that of the so-called elder Brutus in the Capitoline Museum are strikingly close to Donatello's work on the Campanile, Florence. All are distinguished by the same aggressive naturalism, the same alert, stretched, intense look, the same concern with individual character. Even though we know with what concentration Donatello brooded on ancient sculpture, these resemblances cannot be altogether rationally explained. They may be due, like those between Etruscan and medieval Italian bronzes, to the continuance of a tradition which was exceptionally strong in the region that was once Etruria.

The parallels in treatment and feeling between Renaissance painting and the work of antiquity are even more incredible; for antique painting was not, like classical architecture and sculpture, known by actual examples, apart from a few decorative fragments which showed nothing of the immense range of figure compositions and techniques since brought to light at Pompeii, and artists could only rely on the second-hand descriptions of Pliny. In his treatise on painting Alberti relates sculpture to painting and considers that the painter's object should be to create a work in high relief. Mantegna, whose passionate antiquarian interest was as scholarly and meticulous as that of Alberti, actually painted pictures which look like marble reliefs. But although theory, especially the theory of perspective, was one of the main inspirations behind the incomparable development of Renaissance painting, their work showed no sudden infiltration of the new ideas, and like the architecture and sculpture of the early part of the period it was linked with Gothic practice. The chief purpose of Renaissance as of

Gothic painting was to embellish and complete works of architecture. And even when independent portraits and easel pictures began to appear and oil painting was introduced, most churches and public buildings were still adorned with frescoes, and the greatest work of the age, from Masaccio's wall paintings in the Carmine to Michelangelo's *Last Judgement* and Raphael's decorations of the Stanze in the Vatican, are of this kind. Artists continued at first to work within the tradition established in the early Christian period and classical feeling in Masaccio's frescoes is expressed in the sense of aerial space, the departure from the gold ground of Gothic painting, and the largeness, dignity and humanity of his figures rather than in any innovation in the subject matter and narrative sequences of established church decoration.

The familiar story of the evolution of Italian Renaissance painting lies outside the limits of this book. But one aspect of it does bear on the present argument and is worth a passing mention, for the changes in the subject matter of the paintings of the period throw additional light on the relationship of the Renaissance to antiquity. Although in his treatise on the art Alberti recommends only pagan subjects as suitable for pictures, such subjects were slow to appear. And when they did emerge they were at first, like Gozzoli's charming little *Rape of Helen*, now in the London National Gallery, closer in spirit to the *Histoires de Troye* than to the *Aeneid*. Even Botticelli's poetical interpretations of pagan mythology contain an element of medieval allegory. But the pagan pictures of the High Renaissance, works such as Raphael's *Triumph of Galatea*, Titian's *Bacchus and Ariadne*, Veronese's *Rape of Europa*, Giorgione's *Fête Champêtre* or indeed Giulio Romano's decorations in the Palazzo del Te (plate 85) reflect a complete, unperplexed absorption in the classical spirit. All trace of medieval feeling has vanished.

A similar change in attitude is revealed in the architecture of the mature Renaissance. Bramante's Tempietto (plate 86), directly inspired by the circular temples of antiquity, has no connection with the Christian sanctuaries of the Middle Ages. It differs also from the buildings of the first Renaissance period in that it is a perfectly balanced composition without a single superfluous detail. The Italian propensity to elaborate surfaces, to indulge in superabundant sculptural relief, is here subdued to a purity of style which, while it may have little in common with classical architecture as we now know it to have looked when its fragmented remains were entire, lavishly coloured and bristling with statues, perfectly expresses the harmonious ideal sought by Renaissance artists in their pursuit of antiquity.

Bramante's design for the rebuilding of St Peter's partook of the same poise and serenity of spirit. It was an absolutely symmetrical Greek cross design with a huge central dome; but the plan was changed by Michelangelo and the changes made by the ageing genius were deeply significant for future developments. Bramante had planned a hemispherical dome like that of the Pantheon. Michelangelo drew it out to a greater height and supported it on gigantic piers. In its vast scale the design makes something of the same overwhelming impression of grandeur as the colossal remains of antiquity close by. But the classical orders and motifs are used by Michelangelo to create a dynamic, soaring movement which is as alien to the Renaissance calm of Bramante as to the static architecture of the Romans. Like the sculptures in the black and white Medici Chapel (plate 87) whose unquiet forms express an utterly un-pagan spiritual anguish, the great dome is a harbinger of the art of the Baroque.

Certain aspects of the art of Palladio, the man who in his balanced temperament comes nearest to Bramante, also hint at later Baroque developments. Palladio's brilliant chiaroscuro treatment of the façades of both S. Giorgio Maggiore (plate 98) and Il Redentore as a series of pedimented designs receding behind each other, and the illusionist effects of his Teatro Olimpico (plate 96), reveal recognizable Baroque elements – although in the ease with which he used the classical orders and followed Vitruvius, and in the exquisite restraint of his art, Palladio continues and extends the tradition of Bramante. But it would be quite inappropriate to speak of Palladio's works as revivals of Roman architecture. They are the offspring of an individual genius to whom Vitruvius was a burning inspiration in the same way that the mediocre writer of Cosenza, Salandra, fired Milton (as Norman Douglas was the first to point out) with the idea of *Paradise Lost*. They also have the same radiance, they are informed with the same mood of unclouded pagan joy as the pictures of his collaborator Veronese. Roman public buildings are oppressive in their massive scale. Palladio's work, even the Basilica of Vicenza, is always elegant and light in feeling. It is above all in Vicenza that the character of his art can best be seen and felt. There could be no greater contrast to the ancient Rome of the Forum, the Colosseum, the Thermae and the Triumphal Arches than this charming brick and stucco town set in a landscape of meadows and hills; one of which is crowned, as with the temple of a presiding deity, with the famous Rotunda – as unlike any conceivable Roman house as it well could be. Some of the inventive unprecedented features of Palladio's buildings are illustrated and described in the next section (plates 94–99). That he was no copyist but developed and improved on the art of the ancients is apparent in every one of his buildings.

His contemporary, Vignola, equally at home with the Vitruvian rules, applies them in as individual a manner but with a more romantic imagination. His conversion of the remains of an unfinished fortress at Caprarola into the Villa Farnese (plate 88) is one of the great masterpieces of the Renaissance. In the enormous, wonderfully original pentagonal design Vignola preserves the character of a fortress, combining it with a circular inner court which alludes to the Colosseum, Rome. Vignola's garden here and at Villa Lante (plates 89–91) are supreme examples of an art which owed nothing at all to the Middle Ages and was directly inspired by the ruins of Roman gardens. Here the pleasures of the ancient world were revived in a spirit totally unshadowed by the Christian legacy of the Middle Ages. The myths of Arcadia were realized afresh in stone, in artificial grottoes, in fountains and streams. It is surely significant of the obsession of the period with paganism that the builders of both Caprarola and Villa

Lante were prominent churchmen and that the owner of the most elaborate and perhaps the most pagan of all Renaissance gardens, the Villa d'Este, was a man who aspired to become Pope, Cardinal Ippolito d'Este. This amazing garden on the precipitous hillside of Tivoli is animated by the play of five hundred fountains, by every kind of aquatic caprice dear to Renaissance gardeners. Giant river gods lurk in the shade of a vast grotto dripping with the water of three cascades; quicksilver rills sparkle along the balustrades of stairways; broad jets burst from the breasts of great sphinxes; artificial bronze birds twitter in a dazzling torrent pouring from a niche of polychrome stucco, pebble and tufa work; a statue of the Tiburtine Sybil sits at the head of a mammoth waterfall; and, climax of the whole scheme, the Hydraulic Organ, an architectural fantasy like a triumphal arch encrusted with pagan imagery, once filled the air with harmony as water shot from the multiple breasts of a statue of the Ephesian Diana, Goddess of Fecundity, whose likeness appears also on the base of Cellini's Perseus statue in Florence (plate 83). She filled the now empty central niche of the composition but was removed to a more secluded part of the garden as early as 1600. The essentially pagan atmosphere of all these Roman Renaissance gardens is eloquently summed up by the startled exclamation of Queen Christina of Sweden when she visited Caprarola: 'I dare not speak the name of Jesu lest I break the spell.'

The spirit that animates the *Sacro Bosco* at Bomarzo (plate 92) is entirely different from the arcadian mood of Villa Lante and Villa Farnese. This is not so much a pleasure garden as the evocation of an underworld like that of the Etruscans whose tombs overlook the valley in which it is set, an underworld symbolized by the yawning mouth of a grotesque mask staring from a hillside, the gateway to Hell. Nature is not subjected here to plan and symmetry as at Bagnaia and Caprarola. The gigantic rock carvings are distributed haphazard in the coarse grass and untamed thickets of a wild valley. And among the huge urns and gigantic pine cones, the winged dragons, serpents, elephants, hounds, grossly blown-up fish heads, giants and giantesses, sometimes engaged in acts of revolting cruelty, are images which seem to be consciously derived from Etruscan mythology. The gargantuan figure of a woman with an urn on her head whose great twin tails coil like legendary serpents about paths and trees and writhe through the undergrowth, is the majestic Etruscan Scylla encountered on the cinerary urns and in the reliefs of Tyrrhenian tombs; the hybrid monsters with gaping jaws are caricatures of the Etruscan *chimaera*. This nightmare garden engenders a feeling of disorder and oppressive sadness; the pagan magic of Villa Lante and Caprarola have vanished, have yielded to a mood which is curiously like that created with such disparate means by Michelangelo in the Medici Chapel. But perhaps the similarity is not altogether due to chance: Michelangelo knew the Etruscan tombs, for one of his drawings shows the Etruscan god of death with a wolf helmet as he appears in sepulchral frescoes. His art, like that of this haunted garden, foreshadows the coming of an age when religion was once more to be the mainspring of creation.

Notes on the Plates

75
FLORENCE
S. MARIA NOVELLA:
FAÇADE

Leon Battista Alberti was commissioned by the Rucellai family to design a new front for the 13th-century Dominican church. Carried out between 1456 and 1470, it is a later work than Alberti's masterly remodelling of the Duomo at Rimini, and yet less close in spirit to classical antiquity. The splendid façade at Rimini is a bold adaptation of the Arch of Augustus in the same town and achieves an effect of gravity and monumentality with which the noblest Roman work cannot compare. The ravishing S. Maria Novella frontispiece of dull green, pink and ivory-coloured inlaid marbles is ornamental rather than architectural; and the parallel in antiquity is to be sought in the flatly rendered architectural motifs and abstract patterns that adorn the walls of the older Pompeian houses. But Alberti could never have seen Pompeii, which still lay buried. His façade design is proof of the power of an imagination unfettered by set rules and principles. The character of S. Maria Novella and its Florentine setting were entirely different from that of Rimini with its Roman remains. Alberti has brought his Florentine façade into harmony with the Tuscan tradition, established as we have seen in the Romanesque and Gothic periods, of sheathing external walls in patterned marble. He combines the geometrical designs of Florence and Fiesole with the stripes of Pisa, which, marking the pilaster shapes on either side of the composition, look like the notes of a keyboard. Alberti also uses motifs which originated as structural devices, such as the arcading along the lower stage, as two-dimensional decoration. Although the façade is emphatically horizontal, Alberti alludes to the Gothic character of the interior behind it by introducing pointed features in the ornament above the round-headed doors to the right and left of the main entrance and above the very slightly pointed arches of the niches; whilst the circular opening in the centre of the upper stage recalls the prominent wheel-windows of Italian Romanesque façades. The most decorative features of this richly embellished frontispiece, the flanking scrolls, embroidered with the most precise and delicate inlay of conventionalized plant forms, at the same time show Alberti's feeling for architectural composition, for they suggest the connection between nave and aisles inside the church and unify the whole design.

The peculiarly massive, rugged character of the Florentine palace buildings of the Renaissance depends on the use of large blocks of rusticated masonry. These bold, austere structures were inspired by enthusiasm for classical art, yet the style is far removed from strict Vitruvian formula. Looking through the gateway of the Palazzo Riccardi it is apparent that the palace is built round an internal court similar to a Roman atrium surrounded by an arcade. Anyone who has visited Pompeii will at once recognize the resemblance of the plan to that of the typical Pompeian house; in both designs the various rooms are ranged about a cortile or peristyle.

Cosimo de' Medici had invited Brunelleschi to design him a palace in 1430. Brunelleschi's plan was of such grandeur that Cosimo feared it might provoke the envy of his fellow citizens. 'Envy,' he said, according to his biographer Vespasiano, 'is a plant that must not be watered.' So he rejected Brunelleschi's design and chose a more modest project by Michelozzo. Brunelleschi destroyed his model in a rage. Michelozzo's great building may not be so magnificent as the palace Brunelleschi had conceived, yet it is one of the most splendid and solemn of all works of domestic architecture. It was in this palace that Lorenzo the Magnificent kept his brilliant court. The Palazzo was sold in 1659 to the Riccardi family.

76
FLORENCE
PALAZZO
RICCARDI:
ENTRANCE PORTAL

The Strozzi Palace was planned and begun by Benedetto da Maiano in 1489 and continued by Cronaca. All three storeys are rusticated and marked by moulded string courses emphasizing the total effect of horizontality. The unbroken lines of evenly spaced and only very slightly recessed windows, and the string courses, are the only incidents in the stern façade, which is pierced by but a single doorway. The Strozzi Palace would satisfy the most ardent advocate of functional design; not a detail is introduced for mere decorative purpose: every feature is a genuine member of the construction.

77
FLORENCE
PALAZZO STROZZI

In 1465 or 1466 Duke Federigo da Montefeltro, whose astonishing profile is known to us from Piero della Francesca's famous portrait, engaged the Dalmatian architect Luciano Laurana to redesign and extend his palace, or fortress, as it then was. In the patent by which he appointed Laurana sole *capo-maestro* of the work, Federigo described him as a man 'more skilled in architecture founded upon arithmetic and geometry than any in Tuscany, that fountain of architects', and this although Alberti and Michelozzo were still practising and Bramante, a native of his own Duchy of Urbino, was already

78-80
URBINO
DUCAL PALACE

known. The palace dominates the hill town and the surrounding countryside. From down below it looks like a medieval group of spires and towers, but at close quarters it is a characteristically horizontal Renaissance design. It is of cream-coloured limestone and occupies the principal piazza of the town adjacent to a church, the west end of which can be seen in plate 78.

The palace is exceptionally rich in sculptured doorways and chimney-pieces and in marquetry on doors and shutters. In plate 79 is a detail from the chimney-piece of the Sala dei Angeli; the angel was designed by Botticelli, who also made the drawings for the marquetry shown in plate 80. This sumptuous and ingenious work was carried out by Pontelli. The apparently open cupboard containing books, a candle and an hour-glass, and the keyboard instrument against the wall are all *trompe l'œil* effects of perspective. Vasari, who devotes a chapter to the art of intarsia in the introduction to his famous *Lives*, says it originated in the days of Brunelleschi and Benedetto da Maiano. It was regarded by the Italians as a lower form of art than painting, a branch of mosaic. Tarsia is a veneer: two thin sheets of wood, one light and the other dark, about one-sixteenth of an inch thick, are placed together and the pattern is cut through with a fretsaw or a very sharp knife, when the upper layer will drop into the space cut out of the lower. The line given by the thickness of the saw-cut is filled in with the black after the veneer has been glued on to the ground. The Italian *intarsiatore* did not rest satisfied with simple outlines and the next step was to introduce the refinement of shading. This he did in a variety of ways; either by inlaying the shadow in different woods or by scorching the wood or by using chemicals. By this means he was able to depart from the sphere of mere decoration and counterfeit reality. This little room, the smallest in the whole palace, was the Duke's study. A hidden door in the marquetry leads to a loggia with a superb panoramic view.

81, 82
VENICE
S. MARIA DEI
MIRACOLI:
FAÇADE AND
INTERIOR

The church was built in 1481–6 by Pietro Lombardo, one of a family who impressed their personality on Venetian architecture. It takes its name from a miracle-working image of the Virgin which belonged to a wealthy merchant of the city, Francesco Amadi. With its marble casing and its circular ornaments composed of porphyry discs and intersecting borders, this church rivals S. Maria Novella, Florence (plate 75) in decorative charm and gaiety; and though the two buildings have obvious disparities, in the shape of the gable end, for instance, and in the use or absence of sculpture, both are informed by sensitivity to the character of the place in which they stand as well as by knowledge of classical antiquity. S. Maria dei Miracoli is adorned with arcading of a more severely classical type than the arcading of Romanesque and Gothic churches, but, like S. Maria Novella, it preserves the wheel-window of an earlier tradition and the semicircular gable resembles the great arches of the front of St Mark's. Although the façade, designed in two strongly defined stages, does not wholly correspond to the church interior, which consists of but a single storey, it faithfully reflects the structure of the building which is aisleless and crowned by a semicircular roof. The decorative motifs are continued on all four walls of the church so that it looks like a jewel-studded casket.

The interior is lined with slabs of golden-veined marble. The statue on the marble balustrade is the work of either the architect or his son Tullio. The angel is robed in classical draperies and creatures of classical ancestry, sirens and *amorini* sport round the base of the pilaster on the right.

In the foreground of this view from the Loggia dei Lanzi into the Piazza della Signoria is the base of Cellini's *Perseus* commissioned by Cosimo I to commemorate the triumph of a restored despotism over democracy. It was completed in 1554. Cellini describes in his biography how he first made a small wax model for the statue which the Duke examined 'for a long time with ever-growing delight, and then he said, "Benvenuto, my friend, if you were to carry out this little model on a large scale it would be the finest thing in the Piazza." Thereupon I replied, "My most excellent lord, in the Piazza are the works of the great Donatello and the marvellous Michelangelo, the two greatest men since the ancients. Nevertheless, as your most illustrious Excellency is so encouraging to my model, I feel within me the power to do the complete work three times as well!"' The sculptor gives a forceful account of the casting of this statue and of the triumphant conclusion of his labours when, after the chaos and confusion of innumerable frustrations and accidents, including a fire in his workshop, the metal in the furnace liquefied and filled the mould. The *Perseus* still stands in the Loggia dei Lanzi where it was first set up.

The *David* by Michelangelo is a copy of the original, now in the Bargello. The block of marble from which Michelangelo carved the figure was 18 feet high. This splendid piece of stone had been given to Agostino di Duccio some forty years earlier in 1463, and taken from him in 1466 after he had hacked and spoiled the marble with the beginning of a statue of a giant. Since that time it had been lying in the workshops of the Duomo, acquiring the popular name of the 'Giant'. Michelangelo, as Vasari relates, asked the gonfaloniere, Piero Soderini, if he might have the mutilated block and it was given to him as worthless. He turned the 'Giant' into David the Giant-Killer, a symbol of the bold defence and righteous government of Florence. Michelangelo carved the figure in the Duomo workshops and special machinery had to be constructed to move it to the Piazza della Signoria. It occupied the exact spot where the copy now stands. Piero Soderini came to see the statue when it was set up and said he thought the nose too large. Michelangelo mounted the not yet dismantled scaffold and without actually touching his work let a little marble dust fall to the ground. 'Look now,' he said to the gonfaloniere. 'I like it better,' remarked Soderini, 'you have given it life.'

83
DAVID,
BY MICHELANGELO
(*Piazza della Signoria,
Florence*)

Both the austere square and the sober Loggia are full of statuary and here the atmosphere is altogether pagan, even if it could never be mistaken for that of the antique world. Against the wall of the Loggia stand Roman statues of ample matrons, while in front of them scenes of violence are being enacted in marble and bronze. Ajax supports the corpse of Patroclus, a Roman copy of a Greek original; Perseus holds up the dripping head of the Medusa and the severed trunk lies at his feet; Hercules struggles with Nessus, the Centaur, a group by Giambologna, and the remaining space is occupied by the same artist's *Rape of the Sabines* and by P. Fedi's *Rape of Polyxena*. In the Piazza itself the *David* is accompanied by Donatello's *Judith with the head of Holofernes* and by Bandinelli's hideous *Hercules and Cacus*. The total effect, however, is not one of horror but of virility and dignity; the writhing, twisting murderous groups are subordinated to the ordered, classical spirit of the place.

84
CERTOSA OF PAVIA:
DETAIL FROM
FAÇADE

The façade of the Certosa of Pavia was added to an earlier building in 1473 by Borgognone. It is encrusted with realistic sculpture, arabesques, festoons and scroll work (see pages 150–1). This charming little detail of three gossiping youths (minute in size, for the photograph is almost to scale) is one of several tiny reliefs along the base of the frontispiece, which bear no relation to the design as a whole, but are purely personal to the artist.

85
MANTUA
PALAZZO DEL TE:
FRESCO BY GIULIO
ROMANO

The Palazzo del Te, Mantua, was designed and decorated under the direction of Giulio Romano for Federigo Gonzaga, son of Isabella d'Este, between 1525 and 1535. The Palazzo is a quadrangle of brown-gold stone on the edge of the town enclosed by a range of single-storey buildings. It was intended by Federigo for use as a summer-house. Nothing now remains in any of the rooms but the marble fireplaces, the plasterwork and the frescoes by Giulio and his assistants of gods, satyrs, nymphs and Bacchantes rioting over the walls and vaulted ceilings. This one is in the Sala di Psiche. Giulio was a pupil of Raphael, but the influence in these frescoes is that of Michelangelo.

86
THE TEMPIETTO,
BY BRAMANTE
(*S. Pietro in Montorio, Rome*)

The Tempietto was built between 1502 and 1510 and is based on the design of a small Roman circular temple. If Alberti represents the early phase of the Renaissance with its free interpretation of classical antiquity, Bramante initiates a stricter rule. This little building – it measures only 15 feet in interior diameter – has the grandeur of simplicity and complete unity. The Doric peristyle, the drum pierced by alternating windows and shell-headed niches and the surmounting dome with its little ball-topped lantern are in striking contrast to the luxuriant detail and multiplicity of motifs introduced into Renaissance compositions such as the façades of the Certosa of Pavia (plate 84) or of

S. Maria Novella in Florence (plate 75). Even Alberti's imposing frontispiece to S. Andrea at Mantua, conceived as a gigantic triumphal arch, seems restless and over-elaborate beside this harmonious rotunda. It was important for the future development of the Renaissance style not only in Rome, but throughout Italy. The Tempietto almost fills the courtyard of the church and friary built on the spot where, according to an unsubstantiated tradition, St Peter was crucified.

Michelangelo was employed from 1523 to 1531 by the Medici Popes Leo X and Clement VII to build the New Sacristy of the church of S. Lorenzo. The sculpture is an integral part of the architectural design. In a niche above the sarcophagus on which recline the figures of *Day* and *Night* sits Giuliano de' Medici, while on the opposite side of the chapel in a similar niche flanked by coupled pilasters of white marble is the statue of Lorenzo in an attitude of meditation with the recumbent figures of *Dawn* and *Twilight* on the tomb at his feet. This mausoleum surpasses in splendour all buildings of the kind previously known. It is a domed chamber of severe white marble and black Istrian stone and it has all the gravity and substance of Bramante's little building opposite, yet it is informed by a totally different spirit. Here the classical forms are made to interpret a mood that is almost intolerably sombre and fundamentally inharmonious. The two main figures are attired in Roman armour (one of the earliest instances of this strange convention) and this gives a curiously theatrical air to the chapel, as though the classical elements were all seen as stage properties.

87
TOMB OF LORENZO
DE' MEDICI,
BY MICHELANGELO
(*New Sacristy of S. Lorenzo,
Florence*)

The Italians call the figure of Lorenzo 'Il Penseroso'. His face is overshadowed by the beaver of his helmet, leading the poet Samuel Rogers to think it hid a skull. He is the embodiment of oppressive thought and beneath him *Dawn* and *Twilight* symbolize, perhaps, the birth of human souls and their passing into oblivion. Together with their companions *Night* and *Day*, they are also said to express Michelangelo's despair over the fall of the Republic and the triumph of the Medici dynasty. The tradition of the reclining tomb figure derives, of course, from the Etruscans.

The figure of *Dawn* glistens with the highest polish that stone can take, a surface which is repellent to modern taste. *Twilight*, on the other hand, shows everywhere the marks of the chisel; *Night* is rough-hewn, and *Day* is still half imprisoned in the marble block. Michelangelo left Florence before the Medici tombs were finished and although it has often been argued that he preferred fragmentary and incompleted work there can be little doubt that *Dawn* represents his idea of a fully realized piece of sculpture. At one time it was doubted whether the principal figure shown in this photograph commemorated Lorenzo or Giuliano. The sarcophagus was opened in 1875 after it had been noticed that the figure of *Twilight* was slipping from its place; whereupon it was found to contain two bodies almost certainly those of Lorenzo and his supposed son Alessandro who had been murdered by his cousin Lorenzino de' Medici in 1537.

88

CAPRAROLA
VILLA FARNESE:
SPIRAL STAIRCASE

Cardinal Alessandro Farnese commissioned Vignola in 1550 to convert the foundations of an unfinished fortress in the wild country of the Monti Cimini some thirty-five miles to the north-west of Rome into a palace for his retirement. The building, the most splendid of Italian country houses, except for Caserta, is a bastioned pentagon raised up on a platform, surrounded by a moat and enclosing a circular court. Its monumental shape dominates the mysterious wooded landscape in which it is set and dwarfs the village of Caprarola to which it is joined by an ingenious series of steps, ramps and terraces. The interior is so contrived that every room contained within the pentagon formed by the building is regular in shape. The staircase leads up to one of the faces of the pentagon and rests upon paired columns with cornices of the various orders, Doric, Ionic, Corinthian and Composite, following the shallow steps. The walls and ceilings are enriched with frescoed arabesques, allegories and symbolic devices by Antonio Tempesta.

Vignola began his career as a painter and showed himself a master of perspective, but this marvellous staircase, the *Scala Regia*, is more than the work of a mathematical genius: it is the offspring of a poetic imagination which attains an even more moving expression in the gardens both of Caprarola and of Villa Lante.

89

BAGNAIA
VILLA LANTE:
THE QUADRATO

Although the design of Villa Lante is usually ascribed to Vignola, no record exists to confirm the attribution. The garden and its pavilions were created for Cardinal Gianfrancesco Gambara, who was made Apostolic Administrator of Viterbo in 1566. Work on the villa seems to have been started almost at once. Like Caprarola it stands in the region of the Etruscan-haunted Ciminian forests and hills, a fit setting for the moss-grown river gods, nymphs, lions and the prancing Pegasus of this enchanted water-garden.

The Quadrato consists of four parterres, one on each side of an ornate aquatic composition. Four square basins enclosed by low parapets adorned with urns and obelisks surround a circular fountain reached by balustraded walks between the basins. The centre of the fountain is a composition of four life-sized boys (entirely classical in feeling although they are known as *Mori*) standing back to back with lions between them holding aloft the arms of Cardinal Montalto, the 'mounts' and a star, from the many points of which spring jets of water. The figures are carved in the stone of the district which, here always wet and gleaming, is often taken for bronze. The fountain is probably the work of Giambologna. Cardinal Montalto was a nephew of Pope Sixtus V who succeeded to the see of Viterbo on the death of Gambara in 1587. He completed the work on the Villa which had come to a halt after the Quadrato and the upper garden had been laid out and one of the twin pavilions had been built. There were originally eight box parterres, two on each side of the lake. It is thought that they were merged into four at the end of the 17th or early 18th century. The patterns of the eight small parterres were severely geometrical, not the loops and spirals which now move to the same flowing rhythm as Vignola's staircase in plate 88.

The lichen-blotched sphere looms like a decaying moon above the cascade that takes the shape of an elongated crayfish, the Cardinal's rebus, as it flashes down from the terrace above the Quadrato. The whole haunting spirit of this romantic garden is made manifest in the great ball of stone, for the oaks and ilexes and plane trees of the upper garden are no more than a background to a composition which is all stone and water, and which depends for its effect on the geology of the region. The silvery stone of the Ciminian hills contains and reflects the silvery play of water in rim and parapet, and rises from aqueous depths in the form of river gods, dolphins and nereids. It is wonderfully animated by the moss that finds so ready a foothold in its porous surface, and assumes the shape of sheltering walls, appropriately encrusted with fossil shells.

90
BAGNAIA
VILLA LANTE:
BALL-TOPPED
FINIAL

The pagan and aqueous character of Villa Lante is announced immediately inside the gate by this pool with its vigorous winged horse by Giambologna, shell-blowing water sprites and antique-looking busts of maidens on huge consoles.

91
BAGNAIA
VILLA LANTE:
FOUNTAIN OF
PEGASUS

The *Sacro Bosco* is only eight miles from Villa Lante and in the same ghostly region which was for so long the dividing line between Rome and Etruria. This wild garden lies in a boulder-strewn valley below the steep escarpment on which the village of Bomarzo stands, and the sculptures which fill it have been hewn out of the living rock. After having been forsaken for centuries, the valley was turned into a garden by Duke Pierfrancesco Orsini (who preferred to call himself Vicino) in 1560. It is known that Vicino was a friend of Cardinal Madruzzo who owned the Villa Chigi at Soriano nearby, and he must have seen there the giant figure of a woman with goat-legs carved from the rock. This may have inspired the sculpture in the *Sacro Bosco*. Perhaps also the fact that the Duke had just lost his wife Giulia may have influenced the character of this strange garden. There is a tradition that Vignola built the little folly temple at Bomarzo, which is nearly all portico, and certain details of the rock carvings recall the statuary at Caprarola and Villa Lante. The figure of the river god shown here, for instance, resembles the figures of Tiber and Arno at Villa Lante as well as the fountain gods of the *giardino segreto* at Caprarola both in the pose and in the treatment of the hair and beard. And the odd, rounded butterfly-wings of two boys in the *Sacro Bosco* holding a third upside down between them have their counterparts in the wings of the water sprites of the Fountain of Pegasus (plate 91). But such similarities may, of course, be due

92
BOMARZO
'SACRO BOSCO':
RECLINING RIVER
GOD

to conscious imitation with mocking intent and need not necessarily point to one artist for all three gardens.

93
CAPRAROLA
VILLA FARNESE:
TERMINAL FIGURE

The great terminal figures bearing urns and baskets of grapes upon their heads, standing on the highest terraces of the garden alone against the bosky, ravine-scarred landscape or in pairs mysteriously conversing, are the guardians of the Villa Farnese. They are the most impressive of the garden statues and the most pagan. With their goat-like locks and mocking faun faces the male terms make the kind of punning reference, typical of humanist thought, to the name of the village, an Etruscan place after which the villa too is called.

94
VICENZA
THE BASILICA:
GALLERY

The Basilica or Palazzo della Ragione, Vicenza, was an enormous hall covered with a wooden waggon-vault originally built in 1222 and reconstructed in 1444. Palladio was asked to restore the building in 1545. Of the four designs submitted, one was approved in 1549 and the work was started at once although it was not finished until sixty-five years later, thirty-four years after the architect's death.

Palladio has encased the Gothic interior of the Palazzo with two-storeyed arcades, the upper of the Ionic, the lower of the Doric order. The architect was proud of this building, because as he says in his great work *I quattro libri dell'architettura* it may be compared to the works of antiquity. But the noble design shows features for which Palladio could have found no precedent either in the writings of Vitruvius, upon which he based his work, or in any of the Roman buildings he had so closely studied. One of these features is illustrated in the photograph: the side openings of the arches which give lightness and variety to the arcades. This device is not merely decorative; the breadth of the opening is determined by that in the main building behind the colonnade and is uncomfortably wide in proportion to its height. Palladio has overcome the awkwardness of this height by setting the double columns that carry the arch slightly back from the main pier, bridging the space between them by a continuation of its moulding from which the arch springs. So there is constructional significance as well as an artist's imagination in this feature.

95
VICENZA
LOGGIA DEL
CAPITANO:
SIDE WALL

The front of this building, also by Palladio, can be glimpsed through the gallery arch of the Basilica in plate 94. The Loggia was designed in 1579 and with its rich decoration makes an effective contrast to the Basilica, where there is no ornament apart from the simple friezes, balustrades and crowning statues. The Loggia is built entirely of warm red brick except for the stone podium and stone bases of the huge composite columns. It consists of two storeys of arcading supported on massive piers and between each arch great brick pillars run from base to cornice. One side of the Loggia is unfinished. Of the side shown in the photograph, only the lower stage is arched and the opening is flanked by pilasters surmounted by graceful helmeted figures posed against a background which is the most original feature of the whole design. The red brick wall supports an array of white stucco ornament flung across the surface with the exuberance and apparent lack of order we associate with the collages of Rauschenberg or Paolozzi. The Romans sometimes used trophies of arms and scattered pieces of military equipment on their triumphal arches, but never with the vigour and freedom with which Palladio mingles the emblems of battle and victory, breastplates, helmets, greaves, shields and gauntlets, standards, lion heads, swags of fruit, cornucopias and crowns in a wild yet rhythmic swirl.

This remarkable theatre was Palladio's last work and he did not live to see it completed. It was finished by Scamozzi in 1580. The interior of the theatre is built entirely of wood and stucco, with fixed scenery representing the piazza and streets of an antique city in perfect perspective. The sculptures are by Rubini and Albanese. The theatre is candle-lit, the candles being attached to the bases of the statues above the Corinthian columns. In his skilful use of illusion, the brilliance with which he unifies separate spaces by optical devices in this theatre, Palladio anticipates Baroque practice. Palladio's stage setting had a decisive influence on Longhena's conception of the famous S. Maria della Salute, in Venice.

96
VICENZA
TEATRO OLIMPICO:
AUDITORIUM

This path leads between walls of brick and limestone rubble surmounted by statues of nymphs and satyrs to the gate of Palladio's Villa Capra, designed for Paolo Almerico in 1552. The wall on the left is the flat façade of the domestic offices of the Villa which are not included in the plan of the house itself. A chimney of classical form can be seen among the statues on the wall. Immediately opposite the gate is the little private chapel Palladio built for the owner of the Villa. The cartouche over the entrance shows a goat, Almerico's rebus, with nymphs bursting from foliage on either side, while the pediment is crowned with a central statue of the Virgin and with figures of angels which are already decidedly Baroque in feeling. The statues are of stone, the façade of the chapel is of brick coated with stucco. (See also plate 99.)

97
VICENZA
VILLA CAPRA:
THE CHAPEL

The façade of this island church, at once light and majestic, was completed in 1575 by Scamozzi, who like Palladio came from Vicenza, to a design by Palladio dating from fifteen years earlier.

98
VENICE
S. GIORGIO MAGGIORE

Like the Basilica (plate 94), this church shows the architect not merely following classical tradition but continuing it. The motif of the pillared and pedimented temple front is used twice in an outstandingly original composition. It is as though one façade were superimposed upon another, an effect that is enhanced by the two colossal parallel Corinthian cornices, the lower of which, running right across the front, invites the eye to complete the pediment behind the centre gable. This frontispiece with its high-pedestalled columns is not only an ingenious piece of designing already hinting at the later achievements of Baroque architects, it is also fully expressive of the nave and aisles behind it.

99
VICENZA
VILLA CAPRA

Palladio's most celebrated villa, also known as the Rotunda, is romantically situated on the outskirts of the town on a hill in a pastoral wooded landscape to which the temple architecture is peculiarly suited. Palladio found little guidance for the design of private houses in Vitruvius's *De Architectura*; he therefore fashioned them like the houses of the gods. The Rotunda is the earliest design in which the column, hitherto reserved for sacred buildings, was used for domestic architecture. Furthermore, it is built on the plan of a Greek cross, a form previously limited to churches. The villa is a perfect square with pillared porticos like Greek temple fronts on each side and a circular hall with a low dome. The building is of brick coated with stucco and the statues on the pediment are of limestone. No house had ever before been planned in this way, and the influence it exerted was widespread. The Villa Capra was copied by Lord Burlington at Chiswick and by Colin Campbell at Mereworth, Kent.

100
MASER
VILLA BARBARO
FRESCO BY
VERONESE

Villa Barbaro was designed by Palladio and decorated by Veronese, probably soon after 1560. The house was built for Daniele and Marcantonio Barbaro, who belonged to one of the oldest families of Venice. The rooms are grouped about a central cruciform hall and one end of the cross has been divided off to form a square salone, the *Aula*. This is but one of a whole series of rooms, the walls and ceiling of which are wholly covered with frescoes by Paolo Veronese, assisted by G. B. Zelotti. The *Aula* has a coved ceiling, and where it starts Veronese has painted an illusionist balcony containing various members of the Barbaro household. The studious black-clad boy shown here reading a book is Francesco, aged fourteen, one of Marcantonio's sons. The Villa Barbaro is the finest example of the collaboration of Palladio and Veronese. The two men were friends and it was said that Palladio's palaces were like Paolo's pictures without the figures, and that Paolo's pictures were Palladio's buildings peopled with splendid inhabitants.

Plates 75-100

78

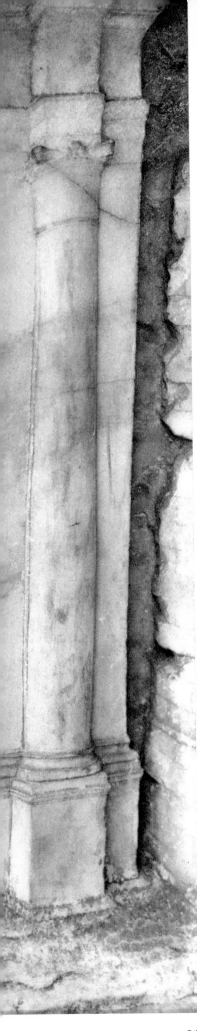

The Baroque Synthesis

Of all the forms assumed by the Italian genius throughout the centuries none in the end makes so great an impact as the Baroque. The sheer abundance alone of Baroque art in Italy is overwhelming. Before the present century it was acknowledged only in passing by art historians and travellers as a decadent, far too prolonged and regrettable phase of the late Renaissance; and some of the most exciting manifestations of the period, especially in Sicily, are the work of artists whose names are still scarcely known. But it is impossible to imagine Italy without the hundreds of spectacular churches which sprang up in response to the resurgence of faith known as the Counter Reformation, or without her palaces, grandiose piazzas and fountains; without indeed the whole scenic art of the 17th and 18th centuries.

Of the three predominant faces of Rome, the ravaged, ruined heart of the ancient Empire, the Baroque city of shrines and palaces, and the complex of late 19th-century and ultra-modern buildings, it is the second, the Rome that took shape under Popes Paul V, Urban VIII, Innocent X and Alexander V, which ultimately determines the remembered image of the Eternal City. And the building which impresses itself most upon the imagination as imbued with a more living, three-dimensional, awe-inspiring quality than any single surviving work of Roman times, is a Baroque creation: Bernini's Piazza of St Peter's, those free-standing colonnades that curve elliptically, then diverge as they advance with impressive ceremony upon the façade of the Basilica, a procession of four-deep individual units, each unit a stupendous column of marble.

The Baroque face of Italy forces itself upon the eye not only as the result of intensive new building on a scale unknown since Roman times but because so many old buildings — even if they were not changed out of all recognition as Borromini transformed the basilican church of S. Giovanni in Laterano or as Flaminio Ponzio reconstructed S. Sebastiano, Rome — were altered, redecorated and refurnished in the 17th-century style. One of the commonest experiences of the Italian church enthusiast is to pass through the portal of some medieval or Renaissance façade, as at S. Spirito, Agrigento (plate 104) and to come upon an interior startlingly animated by the sumptuous ornament and gesticulating sculpture of Baroque art, or to find an astonishing display of gilded stucco roofing in a severe Romanesque nave as at S. Nicola, Bari (plate 53). The Baroque intrudes even into such totally incongruous buildings as the Byzantine 'La Martorana' in Palermo (see page 54) and there is hardly a church without some flaming altarpiece, such as the exuberant stucco tableau of the Coronation of the Virgin in the Gothic *Duomo* of Enna (plate 74), some turbulent chapel such as the Capella Chigi in the unlikely setting of Siena Cathedral, or some agitated statue like that of Alexander III, also at Siena.

The violent upheaval of the Reformation had aroused the Catholic Church to a deep sense of its danger and the faithful were exhorted to abandon the pagan pleasures revived by the Renaissance humanists. The Council of Trent defined the role of art, in accordance with medieval tenets, as a means of instruction in the mysteries of Christianity and the art of the 17th century was jealously supervised in the interests of a religion as ardent and as vigorous as that of the Middle Ages, and practised with an even more burning intensity. The most important movement of the Counter Reformation, St Ignatius Loyola's Society of Jesus, with its practical and psychological approach to the mysteries of faith and its firmness and tenacity in translating into action the decrees of the Council, exercised considerable influence on the development of Baroque art. The Jesuits encouraged extreme realism, emotional intensity and high-pitched drama to whip piety into a state of ecstatic devotion.

But the character of the architecture, sculpture and painting which they promoted was only partly dependent upon their authority and patronage, for it had already been announced by the art of the previous period. Symptoms of a changing attitude, hints at the dynamism and heroic scale of the Baroque had appeared, as we have seen, in Vignola's Villa Farnese, Caprarola, in Michelangelo's design for St Peter's and in his Medici Chapel (plate 87). All these and many other expressions of late Renaissance art are preludes to the later manifestations in stone and paint of the Baroque spirit. The predominantly theatrical nature of this art is merely a particularly concentrated exhibition of an instinctive Italian capacity for scenic presentation which makes itself felt in the products of their genius from the earliest times. It appears in the Roman triumphal arches and their decoration, and in the vast scale and monumentality of Roman buildings. We see it in the elaborate façades set up in front of Romanesque and Gothic churches, in the narrative reliefs of Donatello and Ghiberti, which are already of the same order, though not carried to such extremes of naturalism, as Baroque reliefs like the Vision of S. Andrea Corsini by Foggini in the Carmine, Florence; and in the layout of Renaissance gardens. The illusionist decorations which occur already at Pompeii and are exemplified by Mantegna's ceiling fresco in the Camera degli Sposi in the Castello dei Gonzaga, Mantua, by Correggio's picture of the

Ascension in the dome of the Cathedral of Parma – made to look as if it were open to the sky – and by Veronese's celebrated representation of himself seen as if stepping through a fictitious door at Villa Maser are further instances; so, too, is the genial, high-mettled disregard for taste which enabled Hadrian to add a stone crocodile to the already heterogeneous sculpture of the Canopus at his villa at Tivoli (plate 42); which prompted the sculptor of the *Sacro Bosco*, Bomarzo, to set grotesquely ugly and slightly comic dragons beside his mysterious and melancholy giants and gods; and which turned the frontispiece of the Certosa of Pavia into a riot of ill-assorted ornament and architectural motifs. It was surely this scenic instinct, too, that lay behind the restrained Palladio's unexpected display on the wall of the Loggia del Capitano (plate 95) and made him take such delight in the construction of an actual theatre with make-believe perspectives (plate 96).

Baroque art is not only the climax of this dramatic impulse, it unites all the most salient characteristics of the work of previous periods and all the incompatible tendencies. The innate feeling for classical forms which during the Middle Ages could only show itself in disguise; the love of lavish ornament; the insect-like ingenuity; all these were embraced in the remarkable synthesis known as Baroque, being brought into harmony with the promptings of a conscience educated by the Gospel. Although for one glorious moment that conscience was reconciled with the classical ideal of a joyous natural life, it had cast a shadow over the later Renaissance, imparting to the embodiments of both pagan and Christian themes the curious unease and distortion which historians classify as Mannerism.

This great synthesis in which the whole of the many-sided Italian genius found expression and in which all the separate arts were merged is above all one of illusion. The classical orders and classical motifs which had been resuscitated with so great a burst of energy and inventiveness during the Renaissance period were used by Baroque artists with a heightened urgency and vigour in the service of great scenic creations, the aim of which was to give an appearance of three-dimensional reality to the mysteries of religious passion and revelation. The façades that curve outwards or are drawn inwards into the body of the building, the columns that twist in bulging spirals, the pediments pulled asunder, flanked by writhing scrolls and surmounted by statues in violent motion are nearly always mere screens that bear little or no relation to the plan developed behind them. But they differ from medieval and Renaissance frontispieces not only in the sense of movement conveyed by the curving, flowing forms and the contrasting contours of the designs but, with one or two exceptions, in the way in which the composition is unified. This is achieved by substituting for the repeating units of Renaissance design a bold rhythmic and chiaroscuro conception which controls the whole organization. Palladio applied the classical orders with brilliant originality while adhering to the Vitruvian module, but Baroque architects employ the orders without respect for the module in the interests of a wholly picturesque fluidity.

The façade of Borromini's church of S. Agnese in Piazza Navona (see plate 103) is a compelling example of the freedom of Baroque illusionist design. The composition is so impressive that it is something of a shock to discover that the towers and the great dome are conceived quite independently of the interior which they mask and that this is but another stupendous instance of the screen design. The frontispiece is like a cavern, whose concavity is stressed by the high towers crowning the projecting members on either side. There is no upper stage apart from the towers and the dome, and thus the dome on its tall drum, which rises almost immediately above the pedimented portico, seems to hover above the hollow recess, drawing the faithful into the bowels of the church. The long lines of pilasters and columns on the towers, and the height of the dome, suggest a verticality which accords with the fervour of the religious revival, but this is offset by the exaggerated breadth of the entablature and by the width of the whole building. Borromini in fact achieves an aspiring movement less by actual verticality than by the floating sensation created by the position of the dome, pushed as far forward as possible, and by the loose connection between the towers and the central structure. Even in his Roman church of S. Ivo della Sapienza where the lantern is crowned externally by a sort of spiralling feature of bizarre form, like some oriental ziggurat, the upward movement so excitingly conveyed by the pilasters of the drum, the strange looping, buttress-like features of the stepped shell of the dome and the coupled columns of the lantern leading up to the final flourish of the spiral, is again suggested rather than actual, for the height of the crowning feature is very small in proportion to the rest of the building and its effect is impeded as at S. Agnese by the oversized entablatures and by the immense breadth of the drum. Strong horizontal elements likewise counterbalance the verticality of the much later church of S. Trinità dei Monti (plate 101), and of the tall, narrow façade of Cortona's SS. Domenico e Sisto, with its row of flaming urns capping a classical pediment.

The internal design of Baroque domes exhibits still more clearly the way in which 17th-century architects achieve an effect of soaring motion by the sheer ingenuity of contrived illusion rather than by the actual immensity of height by which Gothic builders strove to express the infinite. Poised above octagonal (S. Lorenzo, Turin; plate 109), elliptical (S. Chiara, Noto), star-shaped (S. Ivo della Sapienza) or even rhomboidal (S. Carlo alle Quattro Fontane) interiors whose concave or convex walls open out into dim recessions, these domes deepen the atmosphere of impenetrable mystery already evoked by the baffling complexity of the ground plans. Guarini's amazing domes at Turin are reproduced here (plates 110 and 111) and described in the accompanying notes. The geometry on which they are based defies analysis: it is the inspired geometry of a deeply religious nature in an age of enthusiasm for harmonious numbers, an enthusiasm which united reason and emotion and regarded the precision of mathematics not as inimical to belief but as part of it. It is characteristic of the consciously intricate structure of these domes that their external appearance should offer no solution to the riddle of their interweaving and dissolving forms. The cupola of the Capella della Santa Sindone (plate 111) assumes the fantastic shape, when seen from the courtyard of the Royal Palace, of a Chinese pagoda.

Borromini's dome of S. Carlo alle Quattro Fontane is another most fascinating example of the illusionist art of creating a sense of infinite recession. It is an oval entirely covered with deep hexagonal and cruciform coffers, that look like the cells of a living organism under the microscope and which diminish in size towards the central lantern until the light from that feature seems to emanate from so remote a source that to the faithful it might well appear divine.

Baroque sculpture and painting are even more intimately associated with architecture than they were in the preceding periods. They assist the rhythm and illusionism of the building itself. The agonies and ecstasies of the saints, the urgent message of the angels, are evoked in the contortions of the figures that crowd in their thousands on the façades of Baroque churches all over Italy; and inside the church the line of demarcation between wall and ceiling vanishes as, in obedience to the painter's magic, the roof opens to reveal a vision of heaven, the apotheosis of a saint, an Ascension or some religious allegory like that of Andrea Pozzo's 'Allegory of the missionary work of the Jesuits' in S. Ignazio, Rome. In this feat of impressive virtuosity the walls of the nave are continued by the painter with absolute conviction to a dizzy roofless height, revealing clouds of flying figures, some floating against the walls themselves, others mounting in impeccable perspective towards infinity. A composition such as this differs from the ceiling frescoes of Mantegna and Correggio mentioned above in that, while they are clearly marked off from the architecture by the heavy rims of the cupolas, it is impossible at S. Ignazio to decide where stone ends and paint begins.

The uncompromising realism of Baroque sculpture and painting accorded with the requirements of both the church and the nature of illusionist art. Of this art Bernini was the supreme master. His Fountain of the Four Rivers (plate 103) is a superb example of all the obvious characteristics of the sculpture of the age: its realism, its vitality and movement, the picturesque reproduction of natural forms such as plants and rocks, and the poetic blurring of the boundary between art and reality; at the same time the whole conception is subordinated to the expression of a definite meaning. This association of art and natural forms reaches the climax of its development at Caserta where the statues at the foot of the great waterfall (plate 123) move freely over the living rock and where the pattern assumed by the foaming torrent against its leafy background is cunningly contrived by means of artificial rocks introduced among the natural boulders over which the water dashes.

The famous St Teresa by Bernini in S. Maria della Vittoria, Rome, is an even more striking illustration of Baroque characteristics. A comparison of this composition with a figure such as Donatello's St Mary Magdalen in the Baptistery, Florence, at once illuminates the extraordinary intention behind the Baroque work. The latter, though individualized, as are all Donatello's sculptures, is a summary of the qualities associated with the saint. Bernini's St Teresa is seen in only one aspect of her nature, at only one moment and that the most important of her career, the moment of divine revelation. So great is the emotional intensity and conviction of this great work that it is impossible to look at it without the profoundly disturbing sensation of having intruded upon a private rapture or without being wrought upon to share the saint's experience. This, of course, was Bernini's aim, as it was that of the illusionist ceiling-painters to dazzle and console the devout with such glimpses of the divine presence as are vouchsafed to saints in ecstasy. There is another, technical aspect of this work which is highly significant of the theatrical nature of Baroque art. The full impact of this sculpture, which is half relief, half three-dimensional, can only be felt if one is standing directly in front of it. Like stage work, it demands a fixed viewpoint. In the same way the Four Rivers Fountain, although it builds up to a masterly whole when viewed from a distance, is most effective when considered as four different compositions each seen from one particular angle. The rock on which the figures are seated, though it is so completely realistic in detail, has been carefully divided by the grottoes into the form of four rough arches with special regard for the four fixed viewpoints that allow the sculptures to make their maximum impact. The statues on the façade of S. Maria Zobenigo, Venice (plate 102), illustrate this matter of the fixed viewpoint very clearly. Photographed as they here are from a point to the right of the frontal position from which they were intended to be seen, it is almost impossible to follow the convulsions of their limbs and to read their poses intelligibly.

The realism of Baroque sculpture and painting not only served to disclose heavenly visions and to create concrete symbols of the power of the Church; it was also instrumental in revealing with an irresistible power the certain end that awaits us all, the pain of mortality from which only faith can deliver us. In S. Francesco a Ripa, Rome, Bernini shows St Lodovica Albertoni in the agonies of death, which are portrayed with horrifying verisimilitude. The saint lies with her head supported on a lace-edged pillow, her body half covered with a sheet hideously crumpled and agitated by the extremity of her suffering. The mouth gasps, the eyes rolling between half-open lids no longer focus, the torso seems to heave and twist before our gaze. If St Teresa invites us to share the bliss of mystic communion, St Lodovica prepares us for the pangs of death. The Dead Christ by the Neapolitan sculptor Sammichele in the Capella Sansevero presents us with a yet more terrifying spectacle, for here the image is a corpse veiled in an almost transparent shroud and on the verge of dissolution. These figures, both masterpieces, are outstanding examples of countless similar representations of the dead and dying to be encountered in Italian churches. Lesser works of art are often still more frighteningly naturalistic. The wax effigies, for instance, of the putrefying corpses of St Catherine and St Agnes in S. Maria dei Angeli, Agrigento, are so convincing that the spectator feels he must take a closer look in order to satisfy himself that they are not real. All imagery of this nature can be seen to derive more or less directly from the Baroque attitude to life and art.

It goes almost without saying that in an age whose paramount aim was to create illusion, minor arts such as that of inlay, in which the Italians had always shown unrivalled dexterity, were pursued with increased virtuosity. The extraordinary decoration of the internal architecture of the church of the Gesuiti in Venice, where coloured inlaid marbles simulate brocade with staggering success, is shown on plate 108. The amazing art of Piffetti is also illustrated in these pages (plate 121). Piffetti was obsessed by the luxurious effects obtainable in furniture by the use of precious inlaid materials. He sometimes carried his passion to extremes which are only saved from vulgarity by the delicate scale of his work; for the minuteness of Piffetti's craftsmanship could not make its dazzling impact except in the concentrated space of a very tiny room, and both his Oratory in the Royal Palace at Turin and his Library in the Quirinale, Rome, amount to little more than commodious closets in size. Floors, ceilings, walls, shelves, mirror frames and the Turin bureau-shaped altar are all adorned with arabesques, floral designs and curious *trompe l'œil* pieces. The consoles in the Quirinale room, for instance, are inlaid with engraved ivory so meticulously counterfeiting stained, dog-eared maps and religious and pagan scenes that the temptation to handle them is irresistible. The contrast between Piffetti's 18th-century illusionism and that of the early Baroque period is indicative of the frivolity that began to invade art when once the high seriousness of the first religious impulse had dwindled. Far from employing his skill to encourage an atmosphere of devotion, Piffetti actually goes out of his way to disguise an oratory as a library.

Decorative marbles play a most important part in fashioning the milieu of splendid ostentation demanded by a theatrical art. The possibilities of gorgeous colour harmonies in this sovereign material have never been more eloquently exploited than in the Baroque period. The indescribably opulent colour of the interior of Guarini's S. Lorenzo (plate 109) is as memorable as its unique plan. The marbles of Caserta, ingeniously chosen to accord with the special character of each apartment and to conjure up strange contrasts of mood, make as overwhelming an impression as the prodigious size of the palace. Blanched lilac and grey marbles change suddenly on passing from one room to the next into darkest green and mulberry; white marble medallions are inlaid in a plum ground and both are reflected in a floor of two shades of fiery red; then these hot tones yield to subtle hues of gold, rose-yellow, amethyst and ivory. In the Sala Regia of the Quirinale, designed by Carlo Maderno, the red, grey and cream-coloured marbles of the floor are inlaid in a geometrical pattern that exactly corresponds to the heavy, irregularly shaped coffers of the gilded ceiling. The effect of the repetition is far more dramatic than that of the carpet designs echoing ceiling lozenges so often found in great houses in northern Europe. For here the glassy surface of the polished marble flings back a reflection of the ceiling, thus projecting a shimmering, shifting counterpart of itself, so that whoever steps on to that magic mirror scarcely knows whether he walks on the floor or the ceiling.

This is but one of innumerable instances of the illusionism which played as momentous a part in the grandiose Baroque conception of the palace as of the church. Perhaps the most ravishing of all secular illusionist decoration is Tiepolo's work in the Salone of Palazzo Labia, shown in plate 120 and described in the accompanying note. Nothing of the apparent structure of these walls and ceilings is what it seems: the spectator is charmed into a world between dream and reality, urged to climb the painted steps out of the light, shining room, to mingle with Cleopatra's retinue, to board the yellow barque from which she has alighted and drowse in the noonday calm and translucence of Tiepolo's magical recessions. Some idea of the marvellously convincing counterfeit architecture of paint and stucco in the ballroom of Juvarra's Stupinigi may be obtained from plate 112. The grandiloquent design of this palace is typically Baroque and yet so entirely individual that it merits a brief examination. The main entrance is approached through two courtyards surrounded by galleries. The second of these takes the form of a vast hexagon, the two farther sides of which converge upon the central oval of the main building. Two corresponding but shorter wings branch from the oval on the opposite, garden side and two additional series of chambers run parallel to these wings from angles in the courtyard. The whole thing makes an eccentric star or snowflake design. It is unique, and yet it is hauntingly similar to the plan of the stupendous complex of the Roman temples at Baalbek; so much so that we can scarcely believe the resemblance to be fortuitous. Yet we have already encountered other affinities between works of classical antiquity and those of Italian masters which could not possibly be attributed to anything but chance and innate sympathy.

The fine scenic layout of Stupinigi is surpassed by that of Caserta which, although it is an 18th-century work, is one of the great expressions of the Baroque spirit. The palace was to have closed a vista bordered with plane trees and stretching for some sixteen miles from Naples to the royal residence in a perfectly straight line; a line which would have been prolonged by the additional two miles of the garden behind the house (see plate 123). The great avenue never materialized beyond the confines of the town, but even as it now exists, surrounded by the concrete blocks of recent years, this mammoth creation of Baroque fantasy still dominates the whole wide plain between Monte Virgo and the sea, an expanse of almost twenty miles. In the bird's-eye view of this plain obtained from the heights of Caserta Vecchia the palace takes on proportions so extravagant and dream-like that it captures the imagination before any of its detail is known. Even Vesuvius, a shape of the softest symmetry rising to the left, is dwarfed and deprived of its magic by the hypnotic attraction of the giant rectangle of the house and the imperious straight sweep of road and water before and behind it. Inside, it is the monumental vestibule cutting right through the width of the huge building and thus permitting the vistas on either side to continue in an unbroken line as through a telescope, that constitutes the most outstanding feature of the design. It moves to a slow, stately rhythm, controlled by three octagons, one at each end and one in the centre, where lofty arches and towering columns yield overlapping, diagonal and receding views of rare beauty into four courtyards. The enormous scale, reducing the human figure to puny insignificance, is continued by the majestic stairway (plate 122), one of the grandest of all Baroque staircase designs. It glides up to a broad landing, then turns abruptly and divides to reach a screen of three tall arches and an upper octagon, repeating the shape of the one below but revealing prospects of greater complexity, enigmatically contracting and expanding and merging into one another as the eye follows the line of arch and pillar.

The great vistas of Caserta resemble those still found in some Baroque cities; for town planning was as much a part of this all-embracing art of display as church and palace construction. Rome, Turin and Catania are but the more obvious examples that spring to mind of cities exhibiting the long, straight vistas of Baroque plans, which had so much in common with those of the Romans; indeed, the design of 17th-century Turin actually revives the original Roman layout. But nearly everywhere the full impact of the plan is marred by later developments. There is, however, one town in Italy where a Baroque layout survives unchanged in all its perfection – Noto (see plates 106 and 107). This city is a complete early-18th-century creation, not a reconstruction like Catania or Acireale. The partial destruction of the old town by an earthquake in 1693 was followed by a terrible outbreak of cholera and it was this which led to the decision to build a wholly new city. The site was selected by Cardinal Giudice and his choice was approved by the Spanish Viceroy. The general plan of this palatial and harmonious town was the work of two engineers, Giovanni Giannoli and Giuseppe Formenti, together with a Jesuit priest, Fra Italia. Noto is laid out on a hillside in a series of terraces forming the main arteries; these are connected to each other by massive flights of steps and dramatically sloping streets. The principal artery, now the Corso Emmanuele, commands magnificent vistas and opens out into handsome squares set with proud palaces and churches. At one end the corso is closed by a lofty triumphal arch, the entrance to the town. It is approached through a rising plantation of cypresses and ilex trees against whose dusky backcloth stand the statues of classical divinities. The two features of Noto that most impress themselves on the memory are the wonderful unity and splendour of the architecture and layout and the colour of the local stone, a warm golden limestone, which forms the material of every building. None of the more squalid aspects of poverty and, as yet, no rash of modern building disturbs the exquisite order of Noto. Pebble-strewn fields begin where its last noble structure ends and even the poor dwell behind façades that look like palaces.

Plate 107 shows the frenzied ornament that enlivens the Villadorata in Noto and which is typical of the decoration glimpsed above many a pilastered doorway and beneath many a swelling balcony in this Baroque town. Its exaggerated character may owe something to Spanish influence, for it is a noticeable feature of Italian Baroque art that its most frantic ornamental forms do not occur in Rome, the city which is as much associated with Baroque as is Florence with Renaissance art, but in the far south where the Spaniards were most strongly entrenched. These Noto brackets are not only flamboyant to an unprecedented degree, they are distinctly pagan in feeling. The creatures of classical mythology – winged horses, nymphs and tritons, sphinxes and sybils – are galvanized here into new and frightening life and convey a mood utterly remote from that of the serene river gods of Villa Lante (plate 90) or that of the bewitching little sirens adorning the pilasters of the Venetian S. Maria dei Miracoli. The pagan deities who had been summoned from their century-long obscurity by the Renaissance humanists could not be altogether banished by the rigours of the Counter Reformation but, in the gardens where they lingered and where men of authority still sought respite and relaxation from the cares of official duties as they had done during the Renaissance, the gods now assumed a decadent, profoundly disquieting aspect as though embodying devilish temptations. The change may be vividly illustrated by a comparison of the great terminal figures at Caserta standing in a charmed semicircle about the lowest of the garden fountains with those at Caprarola (plate 93). Both are intensely alive, but while those of Vignola's garden incorporate a frank, uncomplicated pagan joy, these statues of the Muses with their derisively curling lips are the product of a cynical, disillusioned imagination that is yet extraordinarily potent.

While the images of the gods took on an accentuated sensuality and an air of depravity, many other garden features invented during the Renaissance period were developed with increased ingenuity during the 17th and 18th centuries. In the garden of Villa Torrigiani in Tuscany the popular art of the water joke is elaborated beyond anything found in Renaissance gardens. There is here a little sunken, secret parterre dedicated to Flora who presides over it garlanded with flowers. Whoever walks along the mosaic paths of this plot will find himself suddenly imprisoned by a wall of impenetrable spray from concealed fountains, and if he turns to fly hidden springs will start up at his feet; the very temple of Flora where he may try to find refuge will deluge him with a cascade that was not there before and the goddess herself on the terrace above will send down showers to block the path of escape. In the spectacular garden of Villa Garzoni (plate 114), a truly Baroque invention in its scenic grandeur, a new caprice appears in the form of the bath house where, as in the Thermae of Hadrian's Villa, the guests of the Garzoni could relax, both men and women, screened from each other in their separate enclosures but able to gossip together while listening to an orchestra playing in a hidden gallery.

The garden theatre of Villa Garzoni, like that of the much more entrancing Teatro di Verdura of Villa Marlia (plate 117) peopled in stone by the haunting figures of the *commedia dell'arte*, reflects the overmastering interest of the Baroque in the stage. In one year alone, 1678, it is recorded that one hundred and thirty comedies were performed in private theatres in Rome; and it was during the 17th century that the basic architectural character of the theatre as we know it today was developed. In the theatre, the world of make-believe, the tremendous scenic art of the Baroque could still find expression when Neo-classicism had at last ousted it from architecture, sculpture and painting.

As the fervid sense of purpose which had sustained the great artistic enterprises of the Baroque period weakened, the rhythmic movement of façades and the gestures of statues tossed in a tempest of emotion were stilled and finally gave way to the bloodless form of classicism represented here by the monument Canova designed for Titian and which became his own memorial (plate 130). But a style so congenial to the Italian tempera-ment could never be entirely extinguished and forgotten. A spasmodic stirring of its dynamism lends interest to the calm exteriors of Villa Cordellina and S. Simeone Piccolo (plates 124, 125); Pelagio Palagi almost succeeded in recalling it to vigorous life in his gilded, fairground decorations in the royal palaces of Turin and Naples (plates 126 and 128); and it persists even yet in the popular arts of Italy, in the sculptured funeral car and in the decoration of Sicilian carts.

The majestic yet broken rhythm of the famous Spanish Steps – an upward sweep of three imposing parallel flights changing to the steep, angular movement of two branching arms which meet on a wide balustraded terrace to divide again and mount in two broad curves to the church – is characteristic of an age of great scenic staircases. Both the steps and the twin-towered façade were designed by Francesco de Sanctis in 1723–25 as part of a revival of the great town-planning schemes inaugurated by Sixtus V during the last years of the 16th century. The imposing composition closes an immensely long vista down the long narrow street leading from the Tiber to the Piazza di Spagna at the foot of the steps.

The odd boat-shaped fountain in the foreground was designed by Pietro, father of the famous sculptor Giovanni Lorenzo Bernini. It commemorated the naumachia of Domitian – mock naval battles which took place on an artificial lake that once occupied the site of this piazza.

The obelisk at the top of the stairway was found in the gardens of Sallust and set up in 1789. The incorporation of towers into church design is as characteristic of the Baroque period as it was alien to both medieval and Renaissance Italian architecture. The twin-towered façade was originally a French Romanesque invention.

101
ROME:
SPANISH STEPS
AND S. TRINITÀ
DEI MONTI

With its strong chiaroscuro effects, rich reliefs, agitated sculpture and great broken pediment, this façade is one of the most magnificent examples of Baroque scenic art in Venice. It was built by Giuseppe Sardi in 1680–83. This was the family church of the Barbaro Doges and the sculptured reliefs commemorate the exploits of Giosafatte Barbaro who made a great voyage of discovery towards the end of the 15th century, passing through Muscovy and Armenia to the shores of the Caspian Sea.

102
VENICE:
FAÇADE OF
S. MARIA
ZOBENIGO

103

FIGURE OF THE
NILE, BY BERNINI:
(*Fountain of the Four Rivers,
Piazza Navona, Rome*)

The fountain is a work of Bernini's maturity and like all his sculpture it is informed by a special meaning apart from its aesthetic interest. The personifications of the Four Rivers — the Ganges, the Nile, the Danube and the Río de la Plata — symbolize the four corners of the earth and also the Rivers of Paradise. The dove perched on top of the Egyptian obelisk (a Roman imitation) surmounting the immense rock on which the Rivers are seated, is the emblem of Pope Innocent X, thus proclaiming the universal power of the Church; at the same time, in its more traditional meaning, it embodies the Christian message of divine light and salvation.

Bernini combines picturesque motifs like rock, shells and natural growth with the rush and continuous movement of water and with figures in violent action, to create a new form of poetic sculpture in which there is no sharp demarcation between art and reality. The rock, whose naturalism is intensified by the addition of real moss, grass and weeds to the stone plants, is made of rough travertine which contrasts with the smooth marble of the figures of the Rivers and of the creatures — a lion, a spirited horse, sea snakes and crocodiles — that lurk in four cavernous grottoes between the Rivers and in the pool surrounding the central mass.

In order to be certain of obtaining the commission for this fountain Bernini presented a model in silver of the proposed design to the Pope's sister-in-law, the influential Donna Olimpia Pamphili. The waters were first made to play in the presence of Innocent X in 1651. The figures of the Rivers were not the work of Bernini's own hand but were carried out by various sculptors to his design and under his supervision. The Nile is the work of Giacomo Antonio Fancelli.

The fountain was designed to harmonize with Agnese Borromini's façade of S. Agnese (1633–5), the church which dominates the Piazza Navona. Part of the right-hand tower of this huge front can be seen in the photograph behind the figure of the Nile. The original character of the design is apparent even in this detail: the concave movement which is so significant in this façade, drawing the spectator inwards beneath the conspicuously tall drum and dome as if into a cavern, is revealed by the line of the balustrade.

104

AGRIGENTO, SICILY
S. SPIRITO:
APSE

Sicilians are apt to attribute all the remarkable Baroque stucco work of their churches to Serpotta, and although the author of this dazzling late 17th or early 18th-century composition is unknown, it has much in common with Serpotta's decorations at Palermo; in the Oratory of S. Lorenzo, for instance, or in the Chiesa dell'Ospedale dei Sacerdoti or in the Oratory del Rosario in S. Domenico. The graceful, elongated figures, the charming angels and putti flying eagerly upwards in the path of the gilded rays of a divine effulgence, the dove starting up from a wreath of clouds, are all reminiscent of Serpotta, though this vigorous work, while lacking the conspicuous delicacy and fragility of the Palermo stucco decorations, is less profuse. The tendency of Baroque artists to blur the dividing line between image and reality emerges here not only in the group on the summit of the arch, where Christ leans forward supported by an angel who appears just to have flown up from the body of the church, but in the figure of the censing angel on the lower left who is right outside the scene taking place within the cavity of the arch.

The effect of these swirling shapes of blinding white is heightened by the extreme contrast between this interior decoration and the severe Romanesque façade of the little church. It is a contrast found everywhere in Italy, but especially in the south and in Sicily.

The cathedral of Agrigento recalls many phases in the history of Italian art. It stands on the site of the oldest sanctuary of the ancient Greek acropolis, the Temple of Zeus Polieus. A Roman sarcophagus carved with reliefs illustrating the myth of Phaedra and Hippolytus confronts a huge medieval crucifix at the east end of the interior and this interior shows the work of three distinct periods, not overlaying and merging into each other, as is usually the case, but each occupying a different part of the church. The lofty nave is in the noblest Romanesque style with a carved wooden roof and the crossing, with its smooth round columns and simple arches is Renaissance work of a purity equalled only by that of Bramante. But the eye is all the time distracted from the contemplation of these two contrasting but harmonious structures by the surprising, shocking dazzle of white, gold and exotic colour in the long chancel, all the more concentrated because not a single window breaks the writhing decoration which covers walls and ceiling like a luxuriant creeper. A certain order is imposed on all this exuberance by a series of huge, square Baroque paintings showing scenes from the life of St Paul, but these agitated, diagonal compositions are part of the wild movement of the extraordinary stucco frames which surround them. Angels with deathly white faces, black eyes and gilded locks fly among gigantic yellow daisies, and youths with pale, flashing limbs run at full speed along the bottom of each frame. Enormous volutes, nightmarish flowers, cherubs, lions, urns and nudes terminating in voluptuous foliage spread from the frames across every inch of the wall, covering the pilasters which separate the pictures and proliferating over cornice and vault. No names are attached to either pictures or stucco work, but this decoration differs from that at S. Spirito and also from that of Serpotta in its unparalleled extravagance, its grotesque scale and its use of colour.

105
AGRIGENTO, SICILY
CATHEDRAL:
DECORATION IN
THE CHANCEL

106
NOTO, SICILY
CATHEDRAL

The architecture of Noto (see page 203), completely rebuilt after the earthquake of 11 January 1693, combines the palatial, imposing scale and rich ornament of Baroque design with an element of restraint in actual planning which perhaps derives from the strong sense of the classical past in the island. The façade of this church, with its loosely connected towers, has something in common with that of Borromini's S. Agnese in Rome (see page 198), but here the towers are a stage lower and the effect of the high dome is obscured by the pedimented second stage of the central composition which is conceived as a screen in the traditional Italian fashion. The total impression is one of breadth and horizontality which is not diminished by the upward sweep of the three majestic flights of steps, for they extend in immensely long parallel lines across the full width of the façade. The articulation of the frontispiece with its projecting features supported by free-standing Corinthian columns, its statues of the Apostles and its broad entablature band shows a masterly grasp of chiaroscuro and creates an interesting forward and backward movement, but does not depart from an essentially horizontal conception.

Although begun at the start of the 18th century the cathedral was not completed until 1770. The original architect of this splendid building is unknown, but much of the work executed after 1740 is attributed to the Sicilian master, Vincenzo Sinatra.

107
NOTO, SICILY
PALAZZO
VILLADORATA:
FAÇADE

The remarkable Palazzo Villadorata, like the Cathedral, is conspicuous for the conservatism of its basic design. The façade is a long, low, emphatically horizontal rectangle with a simple main entrance framed by plain Ionic columns and with a light cornice devoid of decoration. But this unassuming composition is merely the background for the most outrageously fantastic sculptural ornament imaginable. The windows are surmounted by curving pediments and broken cornices supported by female heads emerging from great scrolls, and those of the second floor give on to bulging iron balconies resting on rows of figurative corbels of such intensity that they galvanize the whole façade into throbbing life. Cherubim with great black eyes leaning forward from a writhing mass of foliage and fruit, winged chargers whose forelegs terminate in sprays of oak leaves, Moors, Chinamen and winged lions with scaly tails seem to be frantically endeavouring to escape from the stone that holds them.

The palace was built by the Sicilian architect Paolo Labisi, assisted by Vincenzo Sinatra. The sculptors of the brackets were Mulé, Mauceri and Randazzo. The work was begun in 1737 by Don Giacomo Nicolai, who supervised its protracted construction until his death in 1760, when it was continued under his successor Prince Lorenzo Villadorato.

The church was built by Domenico Rossi, 1715–29. The most extraordinary feature of this ornate interior is the way in which the inlaid marbles of walls, pillars and pulpit are made to counterfeit rich brocade, green on white, tightly stretched over the architectural forms or assuming the shapes of curtains and drapings.

The church of the Gesuiti (plate 108), for all the fantasy of its decoration, is not much more Baroque in design than Palladio's S. Giorgio Maggiore. Guarini's S. Lorenzo makes as rich an impression with its lavish use of coloured marbles, red, grey, green, gold, black and white, and with its great volutes and tempestuous angels; but the plan is more impressive than the elaborate texture of this interior. It is basically an octagon, the sides of which curve into the central space. These swelling curves are pierced by big arches with side openings, looking like distorted reflections of those used by Palladio in his Basilica (see page 164). Of the compartments behind, two lead east and west into the chancel and portico, while of the remaining six those to north and south form shallow recesses and those in the diagonals are developed into deep chapels. Through the red marble columns of the openings can be glimpsed white statues in black marble niches, flanking rich altars surmounted by sculpture.

The central part of this curvilinear flowing design is surmounted by the eight-pointed star of the dome shown in plate 110. The chancel is also crowned by a dome which creates a strange interval of light between the central octagon and the high altar.

Guarini, who had entered the Order of the Theatines at the early age of fifteen, had studied theology, architecture and, above all, mathematics, in Rome. His church designs spring from the most elaborate mathematical exercises.

S. Lorenzo was the royal church of Turin and adjoins the Royal Palace, and Guarini began work on it in 1668 though it was not finished until 1687. The foundation stone for a church on this site had been laid long before this time in obedience to a vow made by Emmanuele Filiberto at the Battle of St Quentin (1557).

The design of this octagonal dome by Guarini is as complex as this prodigiously inventive artist's other dome shown in plate 111. But whereas there a sense of mystery is created by a diminishing design receding into infinite distance, here it is the result of a strong pattern of intersecting arcs seen against a diaphanous, dissolving background. The effect is achieved by the number and disposition of the windows, not only in the lantern, but in the dome itself; they are set at odd angles, reflecting as well as transmitting light like the mirrors in a diorama, and laid in an open ring (a unique feature) round the inner octagon of the dome.

111
TURIN
CAPELLA DELLA
SANTA SINDONE:
DOME

The chapel was built for Carlo Emmanuele to contain one of the holiest of relics, the shroud in which the body of Christ was believed to have been wrapped after his descent from the Cross. It belonged to the House of Savoy and had been brought to Turin by Emmanuele Filiberto. The chapel adjoins the Royal Palace and opens into the east end of the Cathedral. It was begun by Castellamonte, but the upper part of the cylindrical structure and the dome are the work of Guarini, and were completed in 1694. The fantastic design is based on multiples of three and on triangular patterns weaving in and out, in and out, ever diminishing in size and leading the eye up to the twelve-pointed star in the lantern, in the centre of which hovers the Holy Dove illumined by twelve oval windows. All the lower part of the chapel is of black marble, while the dome is of grey stone which grows paler with height, thus cleverly creating an illusion of great distance.

112
TURIN
PALACE OF
STUPINIGI:
BALLROOM

The grandiose palace of Stupinigi, designed by Juvarra as a hunting lodge for Vittorio Amedeo II, was begun in 1729. The ballroom or *salone centrale*, forms the centre of a fabulous design described on page 202. Like the *salone* of Palazzo Labia (plate 120), the ballroom, the work of Giambattista Crosato in collaboration with the architect, is a superb piece of illusionism, though here the effect is contrived with the aid of stucco. The busts in the oval recesses are three-dimensional, but the flutes on the piers and on the brackets and the articulation of the walls with shell niches and apparent reliefs of putti and foliage are all counterfeit.

113
ISOLA BELLA
(LAGO MAGGIORE)
THEATRE

Angelo Crivelli began to lay out the island as a garden for Count Carlo Borromeo (of the same family as the saint) in about 1630. It was called after the Countess and was conceived as a floating galleon with a garden shaped like the prow of a ship. After the Count's death his son Vitaliano employed Francesco Castelli and Carlo Fontana to work on the garden. The entire island was eventually converted into an immense pleasure garden with ten terraces. The most fantastic feature of the whole scheme was this so-called theatre. Bursting with gods and goddesses and surmounted by a rampant unicorn, it is the culmination of a design at once romantic and dramatic where white peacocks take their place as inevitably as sculptured deities. It stands on the penultimate terrace of the island.

The site of this romantic garden is a precipitous cliff shaded by firs and ilex, and in the spectacular use the designer has made of its natural surroundings it is reminiscent of the Villa d'Este. The whole composition centres on a great staircase moving up in double zigzags to a terrace, then shooting still higher to terminate in a figure of Fame, with fluttering draperies, blowing a trumpet. The background of dark trees behind her gradually merges with the surrounding landscapes of wooded hills. The pagan figure of a woman with goat feet and horns, instantly reminiscent of the rock-carved goat woman at Soriano (see page 163), sits on a console on the first terrace overlooking a vast panorama. The layout of the garden was begun in 1652 by the Garzoni family who had purchased Collodi Castle from the Republic of Lucca.

114
COLLODI
GARDEN OF VILLA
GARZONI

The theatre was designed by Antonio Selva in 1792. It was burned down in 1836 but completely restored by Meduna in its original style, which is sparkling Rococo, rare in Italy, with a sobering touch of Neo-classicism, due perhaps to Meduna. The horseshoe-shaped auditorium with tiers of boxes and a wide rectangular proscenium arch, of which the Fenice is such an elegant example, made its first appearance in the Teatro Farnese by Gian Battista Aleotti built at Parma between 1618 and 1628.

115
VENICE
FENICE THEATRE

The figure represents a character in the *commedia dell'arte*. Puppet shows were a favourite entertainment in 18th-century Venice, especially at carnival time. The marionette theatre developed parallel with the Italian comedy and they borrowed masks from one another. Puppets operated, like this example, by strings were called *burattini* after Burattino, one of the *commedia dell'arte* masks.

116
PUPPET
EIGHTEENTH
CENTURY
(*Ca' Rezzonico, Venice*)

The villa was built by the family of Orsetti in about 1651. The *Teatro di Verdura*, the most fascinating feature of the garden, was planted some fifty years later. Cut from hedges of clipped yew, it is said to have been designed by Juvarra. Auditorium, wings, conductor's platform, prompter's box, even candle-shades are all shaped from the living green. The stage is a close-shaven lawn and stone figures from the *commedia dell'arte* are half-emerging from arched niches as if to begin one of those impromptu scenes of farce and fantasy for which they were famous.

117
FIGURE OF
PANTALOON
(*'Teatro di Verdura', Villa
Reala di Marlia, near Lucca*)

**118
PULCINELLA,
BY G. D. TIEPOLO**
*(Detail of painting in the
Ca' Rezzonico, Venice)*

The Pulcinella was one of the most popular carnival masks and a favourite subject of G. D. Tiepolo's (son of the more famous Giambattista Tiepolo), who painted them in all kinds of pursuits and made a series of drawings entitled 'La Vita di Pulcinella'. The scene shown here once adorned a room in the artist's own villa at Zianigo, which has been reconstructed on an upper floor of the Ca' Rezzonico. Gian Domenico's abundant vitality, the freedom of his brush strokes and delicate sense of colour are nowhere more apparent than in this remarkable picture in which the theme of a masquerade is treated with the heroic breadth the elder Tiepolo reserved for his epic mythological compositions, combined with a mysterious, poetic, intimate melancholy and nostalgia. In the 18th century Venice became the city of carnival – carnival which began on the first Sunday in October and went on until Lent with a short interval from Christmas Day till Epiphany. The mask shown in Tiepolo's fresco is that usually worn by ladies and gentlemen of rank, a white face adorned with a huge nose shaped like the beak of a bird of prey. Pulcinella wore a tall white conical hat, a wide tunic, and voluminous trousers. This mask existed in Roman times and may have been worn by the Etruscans. Pulcinella's ancestry is bound up with legends of death and sexuality. During carnival, Pulcinellas went about in groups shouting obscene jokes and playing all kinds of pranks. After Pulcinella the most popular masks were those of other characters taken from the *commedia dell'arte*, Arlecchino, Tartaglia, Brighella, Pantalone and Doctor Balanzoni. Women favoured the costumes of Isabella, Colombina and Smeraldina.

**119
VENICE
CA' REZZONICO:
FRESCO BY
G. D. TIEPOLO**

Like the Pulcinella picture, this fresco also adorns the room in the Ca' Rezzonico which is a reconstruction of an apartment in Villa Zianigo. Though the subject is handled with the same breadth, ease and individual sense of composition as the carnival figures, it is more anecdotal in character. It again shows a carnival scene, a group of revellers who are looking at a peepshow. Popular entertainments of this kind first became common during the 17th century and spread from Italy all over Europe. The peepshow had originated as a scientific toy intended to demonstrate the art of perspective, and one of the earliest examples is said to have been constructed by Alberti in 1437. It is characteristic of the fairground peepshows of the Baroque period that they should concentrate on producing an effect of vast distances within the framework of the wooden box. This accounts for the exceptional size of the peepshow in the picture. It is supplied with several lenses so that a number of people can enjoy the spectacle at the same time. A similar peepshow appears in Hogarth's engraving of Bartholomew Fair and an actual, though smaller, example which belonged to King Carlo Alberto can be seen in the Museo del Cinema, Turin.

The palace was built at the beginning of the 18th century by Andrea Cominelli for two brothers, Angelo Mario and Paolo Antonio Labia, who lived in it with their wives and their mother, whose portrait was drawn in pastel by Rosalba Carriera. It was these brothers who commissioned G. B. Tiepolo in 1745 to decorate the Salone, the principal room of the palace. Tiepolo's work is one of the great masterpieces of illusionist art. It is literally impossible to believe, from looking at this photograph, that every architectural feature of this room except the door and window openings – balconies, pilasters, the noble arch, the semicircular doorheads surmounted by reclining figures on the massive brackets – is the work of the brush. Even when one is actually standing in the high, square room, shimmering with the luminosity of Tiepolo's clear, transparent colour, and cannot entirely believe in the fictitious reality of this painted world, the eye surrenders deliciously to it for one magical moment, drawn into the watery recessions of the scene of Antony's meeting with Cleopatra by the painted steps leading into the picture.

This miniature chapel was the work of the cabinet-maker Pietro Piffetti and dates from 1731. As a piece of staggering virtuosity it equals Tiepolo's illusionist architectural painting shown in plate 120, for the walls, ceiling and floor are all minutely inlaid with ivory, mother-of-pearl and exotic woods. The ball and the crucifix are also of inlaid wood and part of Piffetti's work. The altar resembles a writing-table and is flanked by tiers of curving shelves. It is characteristic of Piffetti that he chose to disguise the oratory as a miniature library.

This enormous palace was designed by Luigi Vanvitelli as the central feature of a vast landscape for Charles III, son of Philip V of Spain, who had succeeded the Austrian viceroys as ruler of the two Sicilies in 1734. It was begun in 1752. Each of the mammoth steps of the majestic staircase leading up from the central vestibule is formed of a single block of the Sicilian marble from Trapani, called Lumachella, and the walls are lined with pink and grey marble from Dragoni and Vitulano. The snarling lions are by Tommaso Solari and Paolo Persico, the statues in the niches are the work of Violani and Solari.

Caserta was built by slaves, prisoners captured by the royal navies on the shore of Tripolitania and criminals from the bagnios. It was the last notable enterprise in Europe to be carried out by slave labour (see also pages 202–3).

123
CASERTA
THE CASCADE

The garden at Caserta is a two-mile-long ribbon vista of sparkling water caught between grass verges, leading on and on from the gigantic palace past cascades, fountains and sculptured groups until it is at last closed by a thunderous waterfall rushing like a two-pronged fork of lightning down a wooded hillside from the Carolina aqueduct, specially constructed to bring the water from Monte Taburno more than twenty miles away. The photograph shows the final stages in this aqueous strait-jacket composition, with the cascade of Venus and Adonis and the basin of Diana and Actaeon. These marble tableaux make a most uncanny impression of figures caught in the haphazard attitudes of people playing the game of statues, ready to move the moment they are no longer observed. They have no bases but stride freely across the rocks.

The garden was designed by the architect of the palace, Luigi Vanvitelli. The sculptures cannot be attributed to any one artist, though it is recorded that Tommaso Solari, Paolo Persico, Andrea Violani, Gaetano Solomoni and Angelo Brunelli all worked on the Caserta garden statuary.

124
VILLA CORDELLINA
(*Montecchio Maggiore, near Vicenza*)

This charming stucco-covered house was designed by the Venetian architect Giorgio Massari in 1735–60. The principal room behind the Ionic portico running the whole height of the Villa is decorated with noble frescoes by Tiepolo painted in 1743. The work consists of a ceiling fresco, *The Triumph of the Arts*, and two large wall paintings showing *The Family of Darius before Alexander* and *The Continence of Scipio*. Baroque turbulence seems here to have subsided into the calm of Neo-classicism, leaving, however, a few traces behind it, for instance in the eared architraves of the upper windows which create the illusion of concavity, and in the twisting forms of the sculpture representing classical divinities.

125
VENICE
CHURCH OF
S. SIMEONE
PICCOLO

This church is familiar to every visitor to Venice for it is the first building along the Grand Canal to catch the eye on arrival by train. It was built by Giovanni Scalfarotto in 1718 and combined a Neo-classic portico, like that of a Roman temple, with a sculptured pediment and a dome in the Byzantine style. The exciting feature of the church, introducing an extravagant Baroque element into an apparently static design, is the fantastic disparity in size between the portico and the dome, which makes the church look like a caricature of the Pantheon. Behind the prim, narrow portico and the curious wall behind it the swelling dome resembles a balloon held down by a network of ropes, and seems to tremble on its massive drum.

The Italian royal palaces all contain sumptuous displays of 19th-century decoration. The artist in charge of the extensive alterations and additions to the Palace at Turin under Carlo Alberto between 1834 and 1853 was Pelagio Palagi, originally a painter from Bologna who had studied in Rome. The Throne Room was among the first of the apartments to be reconstructed according to Palagi's design. The railing, whose coils are composed of curling fern fronds, garlands, full quivers, urns, putti and doves, and the throne show how successfully Palagi adapted his own decorations to the robust 17th-century ceiling which he retained: a pattern of gilded coffers, bold masks and rosettes swirling about an oval painting.

126
THRONE AND
GILT-BRONZE
RAILING
(Royal Palace, Turin)

In contrast to the suite of the 17th-century apartments at Turin, redecorated by Pelagio Palagi for Carlo Alberti, the ballroom was all Palagi's invention. He seems to have been prompted to his most lively work when confronted with existing decorations. The ballroom gleams with as great a wealth of gilt and marble as any of the Baroque rooms to which Palagi added 19th-century ornaments and furnishings, but here the impression is of cold and ponderous formality instead of abounding vitality. But the bronze figures of dancers holding up candelabra add a note of gaiety and movement and illustrate Palagi's special gift for designing this kind of ornament.

127
TURIN
ROYAL PALACE:
BALLROOM
MIRROR

Before coming to Turin Pelagio Palagi had worked at Naples with G. Genovesi redecorating the royal apartments for Ferdinand II between 1837 and 1842. The gilded throne with its lion arms is his work while the gilt emblems of the provinces of the Kingdom of Naples and the immense trophies of arms glittering on the enormous frieze are the work of Genovesi. The marble floor inlaid with hexagons of pink and green divided by broad bands of white is but one of the immense series of such floors, exhibiting every variety of geometric pattern in richly coloured marbles, which are among the most striking features of this Bourbon palace. The door of the ante-chamber in the foreground with long uninterrupted panels of Pompeian-influenced decoration set in bottle-green frames is typical of Neapolitan 18th-century work.

128
NAPLES
ROYAL PALACE:
VIEW INTO
THRONE ROOM

129
NAPLES
ROYAL PALACE:
ANTECHAMBER

This apartment still retains some of its 17th-century decoration, and a comparison between the elaborate frame of the mirror and Palagi's work in the Turin Throne Room shows how close the 19th-century artist came to his Baroque predecessors. It is in the original part of the building designed for the Spanish Viceroys by Domenico Fontana from 1600.

130
TWO MOURNERS,
AFTER CANOVA
(*Church of the Frari, Venice*)

The tomb was executed by Canova's pupils in 1827 and reproduces the sculptor's design for a monument to Titian. The death of Baroque dynamism, as of its faith, is proclaimed by the lifelessness and triviality of these figures commemorating an artist who was one of the most powerful influences in the establishment of Neo-classicism.

131
NAPLES
GALLERIE
UMBERTO I

The great Art Nouveau cruciform structure of cast iron and glass was designed in 1890 by E. Rocco with decorations by E. di Mauro. This work of engineering, vast in scale and adorned with gilded Corinthian columns, mosaic paving showing the signs of the Zodiac and lavish stucco ornament including the charming invention of gilded angels (descendants of the Winged Victories of classical art) fluttering against the clear panes of glass in the spandrels of the arches above the crossing, echoes the spirit of ancient Rome. And in the social life of Naples it plays a part similar to that of the Thermae in Rome. Cafés and shops here take the place of the baths, lecture halls and gymnasiums of the Romans, but the Gallerie, like the Thermae, are used as a kind of club for rendezvous and discussion of the news of the day.

Plates 101-131

115

116

117